... and you visited me...

The story of
Prison Fellowship
Scotland

Christian Focus Publications

© 1993 Prison Fellowship, Scotland

ISBN 1 85792 038 4

Published by
Christian Focus Publications Ltd
Geanies House, Fearn, Ross-shire,
IV20 1TW, Scotland, Great Britain.

Printed and bound in Great Britain by
Cox & Wyman Ltd, Reading, Berkshire

Cover design
by
Donna Macleod

All verses quoted from the Bible are from the New International Version, published by Hodder and Stoughton, unless otherwise noted.

Contents

Acknowledgements

The original idea to write this book came from my good friend, the Rev Jock Stein of Carberry Tower. I was touched that a man whose work I admire so much, should think our work in Prison Fellowship was worthy of a book.

I must also thank our dear secretary, Anne McGrory, who typed this manuscript. She is really more like a member of our family and is always there when need arises.

And thinking of family, my husband and children deserve real gratitude for allowing me to take on a whole new family - the extended family of Prison Fellowship. In the early years when our kitchen was the Prison Fellowship office, many a meal was late or interrupted. It wasn't my family's ministry, but they backed me all the way. When I thank them, I am really thanking all the families of all our Prison Fellowship volunteers, without whose support none of us could do what we do.

My husband deserves special thanks. He not only released me to serve God, but he offered his time, talent and resources to enable me. I don't think I fully appreciated this until a 'iifer' made the following comment. Driving home with me for his 'leave out' from prison, he said. "I can't wait to meet your husband. You must have an incredibly trusting relationship for him to allow you to bring an unknown 'lifer' into your home." I have been grateful for that trust ever since.

Lastly, I want to thank my co-authors. Rarely has such a strange combination of authors appeared under one cover - prisoners, prison staff, ex-prisoners and community volunteers. But it symbolises all that Prison Fellowship stands for - a 'team ministry' by individuals from all these groups. The fact that one prison officer spent his day off typing the chapter by one of the inmates he cares for, is entirely typical of the spirit of Prison Fellowship. It never ceases to astound me. I hope you will 'catch' the spirit of Prison Fellowship as you read some amazing stories in this book. Though each is separate, you will see that they are all vital pieces of a jigsaw which refer to each other, and which only God could have put together.

'A bruised reed he will not break ... he will bring forth justice' (Isaiah 42: 3).

PRISON
FELLOWSHIP
SCOTLAND

Christ is building His Kingdom with Earth's broken things. Men want only the strong, the successful, the victorious, the 'unbroken', in building their kingdom: but God is the God of the unsuccessful, of those who have failed. Heaven is filling with earth's broken lives, and there is no *bruised reed* that Christ cannot take and restore to glorious blessedness and beauty. He can take the life crushed by pain or sorrow and make it into a harp whose music shall be all praise. He can lift earth's saddest failure up to Heaven's glory.

J. D. Miller [1904]

FOREWORD

The Holy Spirit is not shy. He is the Hound of Heaven, relentlessly pursuing those the Father is calling to himself. He is the holy Wind who blows where he wills, quickening those who are dead and bringing them to new life in Christ.

The Spirit's inexorable power is not confined to compelling individual men and women; he also calls into being powerful movements throughout history.

Such is the case with Prison Fellowship. This worldwide ministry began not because of a notorious presidential aide who was converted and then started a work among inmates; it began because God himself used the most unlikely of circumstances to bring about a new movement in the prisons for his glory.

No where is this more evident than in Prison Fellowship Scotland. As this book so movingly demonstrates, PF Scotland has not been the work of one individual, but it has been woven together by God himself as a holy tapestry of men and women called to declare his praises in the prisons of Scotland, to demonstrate his love among the least of these, and to show forth the unity of his Holy Spirit among those of diverse cultural and religious backgrounds.

Still, as with any corporate cause, the story of PF Scotland is also the account of individual lives touched by God and then joined with one another. In this book, my dear friend Louise Purvis relates the uncanny way in which she connected with another beloved friend, Sylvia Mary Alison, who had started Prison Fellowship in England; that contact became the spark for Prison Fellowship Scotland. In these pages you'll also read the moving stories of chaplains, prison officials, inmates, ex-prisoners, and volunteers who have invested their lives and energies into this movement. You'll have a sense, as I do, that God himself is at work, building what the Apostle Paul called a *body*, joined and held together, growing and building itself up in love, as each part does its work.

And as you read, I hope you'll be reminded anew of the power of the God we serve, and renew, as I have, your commitment to follow him, wherever he leads. For as we are obedient to his relentless nudge in our lives, he will bring to bear far more than we could ever ask or imagine. Such has been the case with Prison Fellowship Scotland.

Charles W. Colson
March 1993
Washington, D.C.

> God sets the lonely in families, he leads forth
> the prisoners with singing' (Psalm 68:6).

1

FINDING GOD'S FAMILY
by Alan Fraser,
Ex-inmate

On a November night in 1978 I made the biggest mistake of my life. I was out 'on the town' and drinking quite heavily, as usual. Then I ran out of money. But it didn't matter because I knew how to get more - and I didn't care how I got it.

Walking down a dark street I saw someone coming towards me. On the spot I decided I was going to take his money. I was carrying a knife so I set upon the man and stabbed him severely. There was so much hatred in my heart for everybody that I really didn't care what happened to him.

But the laugh was on me - the guy didn't have any money. The only thing he was carrying was a Bible - and he offered it to me. I threw it back at him in disgust.

Later that night I was arrested, and the next day charged with 'possession of an offensive weapon' and 'attempted murder'.

At the time I actually managed to convince myself that I was innocent of the charges. Everybody else was lying - except me, I thought. At the trial I said I had only been defending myself - that Kenneth Macintosh was guilty of attacking me! On the 15th May, 1979, the jury found me guilty of attempted murder and I was sentenced to eight years imprisonment.

As I was leaving the courtroom, Kenneth spoke out. 'I'm sorry you've got such a long sentence,' he said. 'I'll pray for you.' I started my sentence in Aberdeen and later transferred to Perth for three years. Later on I was moved to Dungavel prison - and this was where I began to recognise that God had an interest in my life.

A mate of mine, who had no time for religion himself, encouraged me to go to the Friday Prison Fellowship meeting, because it might give me a chance of getting parole!

I started to go to the meetings, but I was often quite disruptive. Sometimes I said terrible things to the Fellowship leaders, Lorraine and Duncan Ferguson and Pat McCracken, but in the end I began to realise that they loved me anyway. I couldn't understand it - I had never known or been shown that kind of love before.

One Friday evening I told Pat everything that had happened on that November night back in 1978. It didn't change the Christian love that showed in her face. The only thing I can remember her saying was: 'You know enough, Alan.' I knew what she meant.

I went back to the dormitory but I never slept a wink that night. The next day I went down to the chapel, still deeply troubled within myself. I couldn't understand why I suddenly felt so dirty.

'Oh God, help me,' I whispered. 'Make me clean.'

And he did! Deep inside I felt an instant sense of release - release from the past; release from guilt; release from my own thoughts about myself. As I sat there I had a wonderful feeling of actually knowing Jesus and experiencing a relationship with him. There was no doubt in my mind that Jesus had saved me and I knew that he was still alive. Tears just poured down my face and I felt no fear or anxiety at all.

Next day I saw the mate who had told me about the Fellowship group. 'I've become a Christian!' I said excitedly. 'Jesus has forgiven me! And he'll forgive you too...'

'Keep your voice down,' he ordered, 'or they'll put you in a strait-jacket!'

From then on my whole attitude to people started to change. I began to see prison officers and staff as people who needed to know the love of Jesus. I began to love them as God loved me. This came as quite a shock to some of them! They were very suspicious, wondering when the 'act' would finish.

Praise God it was not an act. Something real had happened to me. I became a regular at all the meetings that were held in the chapel. I stopped being disruptive and somehow God made me an encouragement to the group of men who came into the meetings.

I remember speaking to a Radio Clyde presenter who visited the prison. I told her how I came to know Jesus and asked if she would play a request for me because it summed up just the way I felt. It was a song called: 'Love lifted me'.

Being a Christian in prison was not easy. I had opposition from fellow prisoners as well as from prison staff. The staff were still very confused about me. Every time I saw a prison officer I'd say something like: 'It's really good to see you' or 'How are you?' They just didn't know how to handle the 'new' Alan Fraser.

Gradually I made a new circle of friends and, as we spent time together, I found opportunities to speak to them about God. I was delighted when some of them became Christians too.

In due course I was offered 'Training for Freedom' in Craiginches Prison, Aberdeen. But first I was given five days home leave in Aberdeen. During those few days I became very friendly with the leader of the Prison Fellowship Prayer Support Group, Pastor Pearson. I learned a lot from him in our early relationship, though I never dreamt that he would one day be my father-in-law!

He invited me to his church and I soon learned to feel at home there. There were a few problems at first because I was very introverted and ill at ease with people, but God gradually changed that side of me.

I was still on 'Training for Freedom' when I was baptised. That was a really memorable day. When I walked into the church I noticed that Lorraine, Duncan and Pat were all there. During the service, Duncan spoke to the congregation and told them what I was like before I became a Christian.

'I had great reservations about Alan,' he admitted, 'but I have to say that I've never seen so much change in one person's life. I praise God for it.'

My mother and step-father also noticed the change in me and it was the first step in their coming to know Jesus themselves. God's blessing was really evident in my life at that time.

In some ways I didn't feel too enthusiastic about the prospect of moving back to Aberdeen. What had it ever

done for me? I wondered. But just at that time Pastor
Pearson's daughter, Grace and I began to take an interest
in one another. We saw each other frequently during my
'Training for Freedom' period and our relationship grew.
We both became aware of our love for one another and it
was hard on Grace when I had to go back into the prison
hostel. But the time for my release was drawing near!

* * * * *

On Wednesday, 12th September, 1984 I was released
from prison after serving a total of five years and ten
months. I didn't let my excitement show outwardly - in
fact I was so calm that it must have looked as if I didn't
care whether I was out or not. But inside I was full of
God's peace and joy. I knew that I had really been set free
years before, when I asked Christ into my life.

That day God gave me a verse of scripture - 2
Corinthians 5:17: 'Therefore, if anyone is in Christ, he is
a new creation; the old has gone, the new has come.' I
looked forward to a new, different way of life!

I found a flat to stay in and got a job as a gardener with
the District Council - a job I still hold. My relationship
with Grace grew deeper, although we encountered opposition as some well-intentioned people tried to come
between us. But this only served to draw us closer
together and we were engaged on 20th April, 1985,
planning to get married on 7th June, 1986.

In my personal life I became more committed to
studying the Bible, but spiritual maturity did not come
easily and there were a few 'hiccups' along the way. I
made a good few blunders, but both God and his people

were gracious enough to overlook and forgive them all.

What I really wanted was to be part of the local Prison Fellowship group. They held a prayer meeting every month and I looked forward to each one. I soon became an integral part of the group and God used my experience of prison life to help the other members. Unfortunately I wasn't allowed to go into prison with them at the start, and this irked me. I really wanted to go and help prisoners as I had been helped myself by Duncan, Lorraine and Pat in the Prison Fellowship meetings at Dungavel.

After what seemed an eternity I was finally allowed to go back into the prison on Sunday afternoons. God had brought me full circle. He had released me from prison and now he was sending me back in again.

The challenge of telling prison staff and prisoners alike about Jesus really excited me and I found great satisfaction and happiness in what I was doing. Gradually I was able to change the way things were done in the meetings, but I yearned for more to happen. I soon discovered however, that where there was blessing from God, there was also conflict. But we found that, as we prayed, God either removed the hindrance or increased the blessings. I often thought about how the Lord had been merciful to me, and this motivated me to keep on praying for God's mercy for men still in prison.

Prison Fellowship also encourages people to be reconciled with one another. After I found peace with God through Christ, I prayed that I might be reconciled with my victim, Kenneth Mackintosh. He had been praying for me ever since my trial, as he had promised, and I am sure that his prayers for me over the years helped bring about my conversion. I went to see him and asked - and received - his forgiveness for my attack on him.

One day I invited Kenneth to go into prison with the Fellowship team on a Sunday afternoon. He spoke a few words to them and described how he had once been attacked in the street - but without telling the inmates who the attacker had been. Many of the men said angrily that whoever did that to Kenneth should have been severely punished.

Then I stood up. 'I know the guy who attacked Kenneth,' I said. 'It was me!'

Blank amazement showed on all their faces. Many of them had known me for ages as part of the Prison Fellowship group and they had never thought I was capable of such a crime. And now here we were - friends and brothers in Christ! We both knew that only Jesus could have brought about such a change. That was a wonderful experience for me.

The time rapidly came round for our wedding which was attended, not only by members of both our families, but also by members of the Prison Fellowship family from all over Scotland.

I shall always be grateful for the personal counsel and encouragement I received from my parents-in-law and for the way they have accepted me as one of their family. I was glad for my mother too. Not only had she gained the loving son for which she yearned for many years, but she gained a daughter too.

Since then Grace and I, with our family, have been able to welcome many people into our home to help and encourage ex-offenders as well as families of men still serving sentences.

Through Prison Fellowship we have seen blessing

come in many lives and we have been encouraged ourselves as people have continued to pray for our family. One thing I am sure of - as part of his family in Prison Fellowship, I know that God's work for me is not finished yet.

* * * * *

You might not expect to find a clown in prison, but that's how the next character sees himself.

2

CHRIST'S CLOWN
by William 'Billy' Thomson
Inmate

Looking back, I was always the clown, though I couldn't see it. The problem was mates - I never seemed to have any; none that lasted anyway. I used to find them easily enough, but I could never keep them. This problem followed me from primary to secondary school.

I never had any interest in lessons - I just didn't want to know. As I saw it I had years left to learn, so I just went on being the clown both in and out of class. You name it, I was there - the clown.

I could never see that the other kids were not laughing with me, but at me. I thought that, by behaving the way I did, I would be accepted. But it never happened. Looking back, I can see it was all a waste of time. It never did any good. But that was the only way I felt I could play it, even when my parents tried to talk some sense into me.

Finally I did find a small group of guys, seven in all, who accepted me - though at a price. The price was that of being bullied nearly every day. But I saw it as a small price to pay in order to have mates.

School didn't improve for me over the years and I always managed to make excuses for not having done my homework. I used to waffle my way out of situations, especially with my parents, when I had to explain about the bruises I had from being bullied.

By 1987 even I could see that my life was a mess. A Deputy Headmaster tried to help by giving me a Homework Book which had to be signed by my father every night when I had completed my homework. I can't remember how I did it, but I often managed to get my Dad to sign even though I hadn't done the work. Once or twice though, I had to resort to copying my Dad's signature in the book.

I can clearly remember one of those times. Instead of doing the work, which would have taken only half an hour, I sat up in my bed and copied out my Dad's name for about two hours, so that it was perfect enough to put in the much hated book! It was little things like that which made me my own worst enemy, though I couldn't see it.

As I said, I felt my life was in a mess. It seemed to be an unending series of hassles - my mates were giving me a hard time, my parents were jumping on my back for one thing or another, and the education authorities were always trying to get me settled into school. It is only in the last few months that I have realised that they were doing it out of love and concern, not just to give me a hard time.

It was in that same year that I committed a serious crime. After two very brief Sheriff Court appearances I was remanded in custody in a secure unit called Rossie.

I was only on remand a short time before I appeared at the High Court to be convicted and sentenced. I was convicted of taking someone's life. I don't wish to expand on this, except to say that I am now serving a life sentence.

Even after being sentenced, I still didn't realise what damage my actions had caused. For the first three months I just drifted along with prison routine. Then one day the penny dropped!

I was sitting in a classroom doing very little when something made me look at the window. It had bars on it. I looked round the classroom and then back to the bars. At that moment I finally understood that I was going to be 'inside' for a very long time.

I walked out of the room to be confronted by a member of staff in the corridor. I made a feeble attempt at hitting him but I was quickly restrained by two staff members, one of whom I really hated for the next few months. Just the sight of him was enough to trigger me off. Funnily enough I now respect this man a lot. I realise he did all he could to help me.

I spent the next few months in total depression. I found it really hard to cope, both with the thought of the crime I had committed and the prospect of being 'inside' for the rest of my life. I was overwhelmed by a feeling of self-pity and I ended up despising everyone around me, even my family, because they represented freedom. They were the ones who could walk out of the locked door at the end of each visit.

Of course I kept all these thoughts of hate and depression to myself. I never spoke about them because I trusted nobody. So I carried on, screaming within myself, but smiling on the outside. I was a master at hiding my feelings. I still am - only now I'm making a real effort to be more open with people.

Soon after the start of my sentence I was expecting a visit from my family. I hated the thought of it. Like so many inmates I only agreed to see them because I felt it was 'the done thing'. Yet in another way I appreciated their support.

My mum, who was a Christian, left me a couple of books that day. One was called *Run, Baby, Run* and the other *The Cross and the Switchblade*. I didn't know the first thing about Christianity. I was ignorant about the whole thing. I thought it was another denomination - Protestant, Catholic or Christian. Still, I read the book covers and opted for *Run, Baby, Run*. I thought the other would be boring because it seemed to be about God.

When I was about halfway through the book, I started to see that people seemed to be made happy because of this guy called Jesus, so I read right on to the end. This was some accomplishment for me because it was the first book I had ever bothered to read.

For the next few weeks I couldn't get what I'd read out of my mind. Somehow it had really got to me, so I started to read *The Cross and the Switchblade*, hoping it would help me to forget the other book. There again I found I was reading about people who were happy because of this guy called Jesus. So that night I sat up in my bed and asked God to come into my life and help me just as he had helped those people in the books.

Before I had finished praying, I found I had unconsciously slid out of my bed and was on my knees, asking God to forgive me for what I'd done and to take away all my loneliness and depression and help me.

That night in '87 he did help me. It was as if he picked my body and my spirit up off that floor and gave me a peace I had never encountered before. Instead of tears of sadness, I was crying tears of joy, because for the first time in my life, I felt I was loved. Also I felt a real sense of acceptance.

The next morning when I got up I didn't realise what had happened the night before, or what I had done, so I continued with my usual routine. But there was a difference - I felt far happier inside myself.

Maybe it was because I kept everything to myself, as usual, but during the next two years I never once spoke to God again until I was moved to Polmont Young Offenders in January, 1990.

After the initial shock of the move I found I was in a wing where I had the opportunity of working in the surgery as a Passman. It was while I was working in the surgery that I was suddenly confronted by a guy with a grinning face. Jim, who had come from Greenock Prison, stood there and told me that he was a Christian and that Jesus had changed his life.

If he had said it without a genuine smile and eyes which were somehow 'alive', I would have laughed in his face. But he was serious and I knew it. The minute I met him, my mind flashed back to the books I'd read two years before. Now I was actually seeing what Jesus could do to someone. Before I had only read about it. Now I was seeing it in the flesh.

A couple of days later, Jim prayed with me. I went back to my cell that night and asked Jesus to come back into my life. I prayed to God, asking him to forgive me for all the wrong things I'd done and to change me just as he'd changed Jim and all the other people I'd read about.

And as I prayed and asked for forgiveness, it was just as it had been before in 1987 - but with one big difference. This time I had such a strong feeling. It was like a voice saying, 'I'm still here. I haven't gone anywhere'.

When I awoke the next morning and got up, I didn't forget what had happened, or what I had done. Instead of relying on myself, I started relying on Jesus and trusting him as much as I could. The date Jesus came into my life was 6th October, 1990.

That same week I went with Jim to what he called Prison Fellowship. I didn't really know what to expect, but after the first night I was hooked. I felt that I was in the right place at the right time for the first time in my life. With these people around me, I felt that I belonged to something and that I was wanted.

They sang songs and hymns for about thirty minutes and then someone stood up and read a piece from the Bible. After that he started to talk about how he had been 'saved' and that Jesus could change our lives too. A bit later we all broke from the big circle into smaller groups for discussion and questions. It was all very new to me, but I never missed a meeting after that first night.

Since meeting with Prison Fellowship members every week for the last fifteen months, I have come to realise that there is a lot more to Prison Fellowship than a few people who come in for a couple of hours, who speak and praise the Lord, and make the lads feel welcome. It's about men and women, not just in Polmont, but nationally and internationally, who are willing to reach out a hand, to give help and guidance to people both inside prison and out. They are even willing to pick someone up after their release from prison, take them home, feed them and give them clothes. They also help ex-prisoners to find a place to stay and, if necessary, provide furnishings for their home.

In Prison Fellowship God's Word is not just spoken but lived out by the Prison Fellowship volunteers. One of their goals is to try and help both offender and ex-offender to be accepted by society.

I no longer need to play the clown to be accepted, though, like the Apostle Paul, I would gladly be 'a fool for Christ' if that helped others find what I've found.

Postscript

Billy is now in a wing at Polmont where a Bible Class is held every Friday afternoon. Because of his enthusiasm, ten more boys have joined the Bible class and a number have become Christians. Just as Billy was encouraged by Jim in the surgery, so now he is encouraging others to rely on the Lord, and to attend Bible class and the Chaplain's Sunday services. He, like many others, is really fulfilling Chuck Colson's original vision of 'inmates witnessing to other inmates'.

* * * * *

In both of these stories the men mention Prison Fellowship. What exactly is it? When did it start - and how? Louise Purvis will explain ...

> 'Remember those in prison as if you were their fellow prisoners' (Hebrews 13:3).

3

SET FREE
by Louise Purvis,
Co-ordinator of Prison Fellowship Scotland
(1981-1987)

Often, when God starts anything, the beginnings are very small. Nature confirms this - think how tiny some seeds are, yet they can grow into towering trees.

Louise Purvis accompanied her husband when, as Euro MP for Mid Scotland and Fife, he was asked to visit Cornton Vale Prison for Women towards the end of 1980. She thought it was going to be just another routine constituency engagement. She never suspected that God was planting a 'seed' which would grow into a life changing fellowship.

Nor had she expected her own reactions to being in the prison.....

* * * * *

I felt completely at home there. It was the first time I had ever set foot in a prison, yet I felt an instant identification with the women inmates. Could it have anything to do with the fact that I had recently read a book about prisons by an American ex-inmate, Chuck Colson?

These thoughts and questions reeled around in my head long after my visit. The answers weren't easily forthcoming, but it slowly dawned on me that there were other reasons why I should have felt at home in the prison.

On the surface, my background of privilege should have alienated me from the inmates. As an American, our language differences might have blocked all communication. As the wife of a Tory politician, other huge barriers might have been put up. Yet none of these things had happened.

Then I realised that there had been a time when I too had been in a prison - a prison of despair, where fear of death was only matched by fear of life. My despair had been sparked off by extended grief over the deaths of several members of my family. It had set in motion a downward spiral of guilt, self-pity, resentment, broken relationships, a poor self-image and a lack of hope and purpose. I had sunk so low that I was left with two choices - to go under, or to reach up. When I chose to reach up, my small faith met God's great grace reaching down, and I was literally 'set free'.

Within months I found that my despair was replaced by hope; my fear, by faith and peace; my guilt, by forgiveness; my insecurity, by security; my loneliness, by belonging; my lack of self-esteem, by a sense of self-worth; and my lack of purpose was replaced by a desire to discover and follow God's will for my life. For the first time I felt that I was deeply and personally loved by God. All this had happened only two years before.

Now this visit to prison had stirred up these memories of my subconscious 'prison experience', giving me this unexpected sense of oneness with the inmates. And I wondered - hadn't the same kind of problems and failed solutions sent us all to our various prisons in the first place? And if I had found from my own experience that a personal relationship with God had led to total rehabilitation - couldn't it work for other prisoners as well?

These thoughts were much on my mind as I wrote my thank you letter to the Prison Governor. I mentioned the book *Born Again* by Chuck Colson, which told of his conversion and the founding of Prison Fellowship in the United States. I also asked whether there might be a place for such a ministry in the prisons of Scotland - never dreaming what the outcome would be!

A few weeks later another important part of God's plan was revealed to me, though of course I didn't recognise it as such at the time. Someone sent me a tape by Sylvia Mary Alison, the wife of a Westminster MP. On the tape she spoke about two things which really stirred my heart. One was her beginning a Wives' Parliamentary Prayer Group at Westminster, and the other was her founding of Prison Fellowship in England and Wales.

I couldn't wait to talk to her! But how? You don't just phone such a busy and important lady and ask to meet. So I wrote her a letter, telling her of my interest in both the Parliamentary Prayer group and Prison Fellowship. Somehow though, I didn't have the nerve to post the letter, and it sat in my kitchen day after day.

Then one morning the telephone rang. It was the secretary of the local Christian Coffee Club. She asked me, since I was the wife of an MP, if I would mind inviting the wife of another MP to speak to their Coffee Club?

I said I would happily do so and asked what the lady's

name was. Sylvia Mary Alison! So I amended my letter and invited her to come and stay with me for three days in June, 1981.

Sylvia Mary's visit changed many lives in Scotland. For me personally, it was the beginning of a friendship and an adventure which was to take us to many countries together and provide rich fellowship.

During her stay she spoke at the Christian Coffee Club and to our 'Lydia' intercessory prayer group. The things she said prompted my husband and a few other Euro-MPs from all parties, nationalities and denominations to start a Prayer Breakfast in the European Parliament. This continues to the present day under the leadership of Sir Fred Catherwood, a former Vice President of the European Parliament.

But the most significant part of her visit was when she addressed a day-long meeting in my home. We had invited people whom we felt might be interested in starting Prison Fellowship in Scotland, and about twenty attended.

Some had been present at the early meetings of Prison Fellowship in England, where they had heard Chuck Colson speak. Many were members of prison staff, who from their front line vantage point, could see the need for Christians to be involved with prisoners.

Sylvia Mary outlined Chuck Colson's main programme for Prison Fellowship in the United States. This was to send Christian lay people into prisons to hold seminars; to bring Christian inmates out of prisons in pairs for discipleship training; and to send these inmates back into the prisons to finish their sentences 'as Christian "cell leaders", sharing their faith with other prisoners.' [1] The concept of inmates reaching out to other inmates was really exciting to most of us present that day.

She then went on to describe how Prison Fellowship had developed in England out of small prayer groups, all relating to a central 'core group'. She also told us about her own vision of 'the house' she felt God was building through Prison Fellowship, reminding us that 'except the LORD build the house, they labour in vain that build it' (Psalm 127:1).

God really challenged us that day through Sylvia Mary. By the end of the meeting a small 'core group' emerged to take responsibility for Prison Fellowship Scotland. We came from every denomination and background. Apart from myself, once an Episcopalian and now a member of the Church of Scotland, there were: Angus Creighton - a Baptist prison social worker; Hamish Ross - a Brethren Assistant Prison Governor; Derek Watt - a Brethren Prison Officer; John Marsburgh - a Baptist Prison Officer; and Helena Bryce - a prison social worker from the Free Church of Scotland.

To this core group we co-opted a Church of Scotland Senior Prison Chaplain, a Roman Catholic Prison Officer, experienced Prison Visitors, and an ex-prisoner - all from different denominations!

I agreed to become the 'postbag' for Prison Fellowship Scotland. At first it seemed a passive title, but I soon became quite active. In July a letter arrived from Prison Fellowship International in Washington, saying that Chuck Colson was coming to Scotland in mid-November! He had asked William Fitch from Prison Fellowship

---

1. From *God is Building a House* by Sylvia Mary Alison p.37 by kind permission of Harper Collins

Northern Ireland to organise the visit.

We moved into high gear at once, and asked for Alex Allan's help. He and his wife had long been running Bible Classes at Glenochil Detention Centre and Young Offenders' Institution. Alex not only gave us wise advice, but attended several crucial meetings in those early days. He was eager that Prison Fellowship should be run on a Scottish basis, and that we should include Carstairs State Hospital - which we did.

We looked upon him as a representative of all the wonderful Bible Class leaders who had been working faithfully in Scottish prisons for many years. We respected them and their commitment enormously and wanted to share their work load. Some of them were understandably uneasy about certain aspects of Prison Fellowship in the early days, but as time has gone on we have developed a good working relationship with them. Our current Chairman, Jack Keenan, continues to lead a Bible Class team at Low Moss Prison, where he has been involved for many years.

Then, early in September, two Senior Prison Governors - Mr. William McVey and a colleague - asked to meet me. They wanted to find out just what this new group called Prison Fellowship was all about. At that point I barely knew what it was all about myself! But that meeting confirmed to me that God really does use 'the weak and foolish things of the world to shame the wise' and accomplish his goals.

I invited them to my home for dinner and we had barely begun our conversation about Prison Fellowship, when I choked on a fish bone and had to disappear, gagging, from the table! I thought that was the end of me

33

and of Prison Fellowship! I could hardly speak for the rest of the evening, so the two governors were left to do most of the talking. Perhaps that was God's way of shutting me up and getting them involved!

They felt it was important that the members of our core group should meet with the Church of Scotland's Home Mission Department, as they appointed all the Senior Prison Chaplains. They also advised us to meet the Director of the Scottish Prison Service.

Governor McVey said that he was happy to be used as a reference, and that I should 'just call him' whenever I needed advice or help. He may have regretted that offer over the next ten years as letters, memos and telephone calls poured in from me. But if so, he never showed any sign of it and he always went above and beyond the call of duty to help get Prison Fellowship off the ground. His friendship and help over the years were really important to Prison Fellowship.

In mid-September we met the Home Mission Board and agreed to tell the Chaplains about Prison Fellowship at the forthcoming Prison Chaplains' Conference. Our spokesman at the Conference was a Senior Prison Chaplain - a member of our core group. Some of the Prison Chaplains could not see the need for Prison Fellowship, while others feared that to introduce well-meaning but untrained Christian lay people into prisons might cause difficulties.

Our spokesman assured them that Prison Fellowship aimed to come under the Chaplains' authority and to assist them. Since then we have tried to have a Chaplain on our Board of Trustees to increase communication and understanding.

Later that same day we had our first planning meeting for Chuck Colson's November visit. William Fitch, from Prison Fellowship Northern Ireland, was in charge. He approved the steps we had already taken to implement the setting up of Prison Fellowship in Scotland. It was a prayerful meeting and within two hours Chuck's Scottish itinerary was finalised.

During our coffee break, a few of us went to the Church of Scotland Bookshop where Catherine Marshall was signing copies of her latest book. She had been influential in my own conversion so I was thrilled to meet her. She was a West Virginian who had married a Scot - just like myself.

When I told her that a group of us was currently setting up Prison Fellowship in Scotland, she was delighted and told us how she had been among the early supporters of Prison Fellowship in the United States! She took my name and said she would pray for the rest of our meeting. That was a red-letter day for me, confirming as it did, my sense of God's leading in this venture.

We ended the day with a visit to Dungavel Prison where a group of Christians, who had been working in the prison for some time (and whose story you can read in the next chapter!) showed me the great potential for Prison Fellowship.

The atmosphere in the Prison Chapel was electric - I don't know whether the inmates or the visitors were the more blessed by the evening. That impression of mutual blessing still comes to me every time I go into prison for fellowship.

A week later some of our core group met Mr. Kenneth Forbes, the Director of the Scottish Prison Service.

Typically, Governor Bill McVey arranged to be present to ease the way for us. Mr. Forbes welcomed our initiative and agreed to write a letter of introduction for Prison Fellowship to all the Prison Governors in Scotland. In this letter he encouraged them to attend the luncheon we were giving for Chuck Colson in November. He advised us to proceed cautiously and to work through Prison Governors and Chaplains, which we willingly agreed to do.

It was the first of many occasions when we realised how many senior staff members in the Prison Service saw the need for Christian involvement in prisons. Looking back, I can see the providence of God at work in placing a dedicated Christian like Kenneth Forbes in that key position at that crucial time. He opened many doors for us. Four months later he died.

Each succeeding Director and Deputy Director has backed our work. However, Kenneth Forbes and Bill McVey were the pioneers, the risk takers. They really embodied the Scottish Prison Service motto: 'Dare to Care'.

A week after meeting the Director, some of the core group met one of the leaders of the Roman Catholic Church in Scotland. We wanted to encourage Catholic support for Prison Fellowship. We felt God's calling was to reach the whole prison population through all Christian denominations in Scotland. As a large part of the prison population was Roman Catholic, we felt we both wanted and needed the involvement of the Roman Catholic Church in the undertaking. Hence our early meeting with the Catholic Church leader.

This policy was not without cost to us, due to the religious divisions in Scotland. But ten years later we are still convinced that it is the policy that Jesus would have followed. We have had the support of some wonderful Catholic volunteers whose presence with us has strengthened our witness and brought reconciliation between Catholics and Protestants in the prisons.

When we first started taking fellowship groups into prison I was shocked to learn that many Catholic inmates did not believe that Protestants could be Christians, and vice versa! In every prison where we work, Catholics and Protestants are equally welcome and in no way encouraged to change their church affiliation.

During October and November it was 'all systems go' preparing for Chuck Colson's visit. By the time he arrived we had a heavy schedule of events planned for him. It started with a conference for Prison Chaplains at which Chuck spoke and answered questions. We were grateful that thirty chaplains from all over Scotland took the trouble to attend.

The meeting was constructive and gave the chaplains the chance to express any doubts they felt about Prison Fellowship. It was, however, difficult to argue with the proven track record of Prison Fellowship in the United States. William Fitch and Anthony Cordle were also present and told of the positive things which had been happening in Prison Fellowships in Northern Ireland, England and Wales.

After the Chaplains' meeting, Chuck had lunch with most of the Prison Governors of Scotland. When he later spoke and answered questions, almost all of them were receptive to his ideas and their support for Prison Fellowship has increased since that day, making our work so much easier.

Later Chuck met over a hundred potential Prison Fellowship volunteers, most of whom are still working with us ten years later. He also addressed a meeting sponsored by the Christian Coffee Clubs of Scotland to which busloads of men and women poured in from all over the country. He spoke in an inspired and challenging way and since that time some of the Christian Coffee Clubs have 'adopted' a prison, into which they send Christian books. As a result some inmates have turned to Jesus through reading alone in their cells.

The next day Chuck spoke to hundreds of people in the Tron Church in Glasgow. It was there that our present Director had his first introduction to Prison Fellowship.

Chuck finished his first tour with a rousing evening in the chapel at Dungavel Prison, and we all felt elated but sad to say our goodbyes to Chuck that night.

Life might have seemed rather flat after Chuck's visit had there not been so much follow-up work to do. Letters began to arrive from potential volunteers and our little office became much busier. Chuck Colson had smiled when he saw the cardboard box I'd been using as my filing cabinet. We were soon to outgrow that!

As the work grew, God provided vital secretarial help for me.

First he sent Marcia, a lovely American lady, who not only coped with office duties but accompanied me on speaking engagements. She was spiritually mature, and we often prayed together when we needed to know God's way forward in any situation. She is now a missionary in Malawi, but I thank God for sending her briefly to Scotland at just the right time to help.

Later God sent me another wonderful secretary from

my own prayer group. Heather started praying about our need for a secretary and then discovered that she was the answer to her own prayers! A gifted musician, she felt clear guidance that she was to take a typing course and do all the menial tasks in our office.

Once again the Lord made wonderful provision for our needs for, although we did not have any income for staff salaries, God kept sending volunteer help of the highest possible standard. Consequently our budget for that first year was only £150.

Our first task was to set up prayer support groups around Scotland. Our goal was to have one such group for each prison in the country. We felt that prayer was the starting point and single most important priority in our ministry.

So, in twos and threes, members of the core group joined me in touring the country to set up these groups. I felt humbled by the way prison staff members gave up their free evenings and holidays to come with me, convinced, as I was, of the importance of prayer.

During the next few months we put together a Board of Trustees, elected office bearers and set up a Charitable Trust. Again, the Lord called together men and women of excellence from every Christian denomination. I was asked to co-ordinate the work. The fact that we began with no paid staff meant that we worked very much as a team.

When, after six years, the work outgrew my capacity to cope, our first director, Colin Cuthbert, was delighted to carry on leading a 'team' ministry. Again, he was God's man at God's time for the job - as you'll read in Chapter Seventeen.

For me those first few years of setting up Prison Fellowship were some of the most exciting, demanding and fulfilling years ever. Looking back on it, I know the Lord must have given me the strength to fit everything in, as I was also trying to share my husband's political work in his huge Euro-Constituency, representing 560,000 people.

Life was never predictable. One night I would be in a prison and the following night in a palace. Sometimes I had to choose between the two, and my preference would almost always be for the prison. This showed me how much the Lord had changed my priorities.

Meanwhile I was also trying to be a good mother to my three teenage children. There were times when I put my allegiance to Prison Fellowship ahead of my family, which I now realise was wrong. This is a real danger for people in Christian work.

Yet I think my family received more from my involvement with Prison Fellowship than they lost. They really enjoyed having inmates on 'Training for Freedom' and ex-inmates come to stay with us. Once we had an inmate with us for Christmas. He hadn't spent a Christmas outside prison for ten years and seeing his enjoyment really made that Christmas special for all my family.

Every Christmas I receive telephone calls from prisoners and ex-prisoners. Some are happy but some are sad. One year, an hour before Christmas dinner, I had a call from an ex-inmate from Cornton Vale. She said she was going to kill herself. I was in Fife and she was in Edinburgh. Within half an hour Prison Fellowship volunteers were ministering to her needs. How thankful I was for our 'extended family' network! About three months later this same girl 'phoned. Her voice was changed, softer. She told me she finally understood how much God loved her, and that the Bible had 'come alive' for her. Six months later she died. I was glad to know that at least she was safe for eternity.

In September 1991, we returned to the Tron Church, Glasgow, to celebrate our tenth anniversary. We wanted to look back and give thanks for what God had done through Prison Fellowship during those years. It was a special blessing to have Chuck Colson with us again, along with brothers and sisters in Prison Fellowship ministries from every continent. They reminded us that Prison Fellowship is not so much an organisation, as a movement of God all over the world. We all consider each other 'family'.

My only regret that evening was that I had to speak from the pulpit of the Tron with a black eye! I wondered what kind of witness I made for the Lord. It was typical of his graciousness that he let me know it was okay by sending an ex-inmate from Cornton Vale to speak to me. She also had a black eye. She said how comforted she was to know that people like me had black eyes too! I don't think she really believed my explanation that I had got mine from a fall, but in a strange way, I felt she was paying me a compliment.

Perhaps it was symbolic that, after ten years of my identification with the inmates, they - for all the wrong reasons - were at last identifying with me. Background and accents apart, she reminded me yet again that we are all equal and precious at the foot of the Cross.

I thank God for sending me into prison all those years ago to discover this. Whenever I go there, it is still truly a homecoming for me. I feel like a 'fellow prisoner', but one among many, who is at last set free.

* * * * *

But how do Prison Fellowship groups work out in practice? What sort of people volunteer to help? How do they get started? God sometimes prepares the ground by using people like Lorraine Ferguson whose group preceded Prison Fellowship - as you will read ...

> 'Unless the LORD builds the house,
> its builders labour in vain' (Psalm 127:1).

Chapter Four

PIONEERING PRISON FELLOWSHIP
Lorraine Ferguson
Prison Fellowship Volunteer,
H.M. Prison, Dungavel

Pat McCracken had been a Christian for only a short time when she was asked to take lunch to inmates who were painting the local church in Strathaven. There she recognised a young man who, ten years earlier, had been found guilty of a Lanarkshire murder. Pat had been reporting on the case for her local newspaper at the time.

Somewhat disturbed by this, she thought about all she had done in those years. She had married, started a family, and, most importantly, become a Christian. On her conversion one of the verses which had great meaning for her was: 'If the Son sets you free, you will be free indeed'. If only, when Dungavel's gates opened to set the prisoners free, they were really free in the Christian sense of the word!

* * * * *

Dungavel, a medium security prison, is situated eight miles from Strathaven in Lanarkshire. It houses one hundred and forty seven men, mostly long-term prisoners. Having served their earlier years at maximum security prisons, they go to Dungavel for the last years of their sentence.

Just four miles from the prison, at a ladies' Bible study group, Pat told her fellow members about meeting the prisoner.

'Wouldn't it be wonderful' she said, 'if they could have meetings like ours inside the prison?'

For months, Pat and her friends prayed about the idea and in the end they decided to ask the authorities if they could send in Christian books for the prisoners. Pat went to see the woman Governor and she gave permission in principle, if the Chaplain agreed. The Chaplain was new to the area and only too pleased to have help with the spiritual input to the prison.

So the books started going in, and it wasn't long before another opportunity arose. Hamilton Church had hired the film *Joni*, and they offered to show it at the prison. Again permission was granted. Church volunteers and inmates watched together and afterwards intermingled to talk about Joni's faith. This had helped her, a hopeless and helpless paraplegic, to become a strong and beautiful ambassador for Jesus, even though she is still 'imprisoned' in her wheelchair.

The inmates' interest had definitely been stirred, but what was the next step? Pat still longed for a discussion group in the prison, but so many people had tried to put her off.

'Women in a male prison?', they questioned. But the Bible study ladies prayed again following the Joni film, and Pat made another appointment to see the Governor.

Before Pat could even open her mouth the Governor

said she felt it was time a discussion group was started in the prison!

'What we need is a team of willing helpers,' she added.

Pat eagerly agreed to find some. And this is the point at which I became involved. Pat asked me, and a man called Bill Black, if we would help get the group started. We felt the format should be the same as that of a home Bible study - relaxed and informal - so that the men would feel at ease and free to ask questions. And we decided to meet on Friday nights as it would suit inmates, prison staff and ourselves.

Bill, Pat and I were so enthusiastic after our first visit that my husband Duncan's curiosity was aroused.

'How can you possibly enjoy giving up your Friday nights to spend time in a prison?' he asked.

Nevertheless when he came with us a few weeks later he found himself not only spending Friday evenings at Dungavel, but being challenged and blessed, in spite of his initial reservations. Later Jimmy Burns, who was already working in the prison through AA, joined us, and many others have come along since then.

There was such great interest among the men, and we were granted so much freedom by the authorities, that several different groups emerged. Dave McKinlay held an in-depth study on Tuesday evenings; we had an informal question time on Sunday afternoons; and Jimmy Burns and Brother Paul led a prayer and praise group on Wednesday evenings.

The men who became Christians were discipled inside the prison, until the time came for them to transfer to open prisons. Afterwards we tried to maintain contact through letters and visits. But we soon discovered other needs. On release, men needed help with furnishing flats and finding employment, as well as friendship and Christian fellowship. The Social Work department and prison staff did what they could, but more was obviously needed to meet the increased demands.

In God's timing, it was at that precise moment that Chuck Colson paid a visit to Scotland and, at a meeting in Edinburgh, he told prison governors about the work of Prison Fellowship in America. The next day the governor of Dungavel wrote and asked the Chaplains and 'the Friday group' to meet her. Prison Fellowship Scotland was inaugurated at that meeting.

Prison Fellowship had clear aims. We were already praying and teaching Christian beliefs through Bible studies and discussion. The weak area was linking prisoners, ex-prisoners and their families with caring Christians outside the prison. By becoming part of Prison Fellowship Scotland we now had contact with prisons and volunteers all over Scotland and even further afield. When prisoners moved to other prisons we could telephone the Prison Fellowship group working there.

Rosemary was a case in point. Her home was near Birmingham and she had previously stayed with Prison Fellowship volunteers Eddie and Frankie Macguire when her husband, Harry, was in Perth prison. When he was transferred to Dungavel, Frankie phoned to ask if we could find a place for her. Rosemary became part of the extended Prison Fellowship family and stayed with us one weekend a month over the next two years. Harry has now been released and has joined Rosemary in her local church, where he is involved in Bible study courses.

Sometimes we needed other kinds of help from the Prison Fellowship network. Mark was creating problems within the group by asking awkward questions. He had read widely, searching for the truth in Buddhism, Hinduism and every other 'ism'. We were out of our depth! So we asked the Lord to help.

He set things in motion at one of the Prison Fellowship's Open Days. These are held every year in the Christian Centre in Bishopbriggs, where the Prison Fellowship office is located. Everybody tries to attend: ex-inmates, serving inmates from Open Prisons, volunteers, prison staff. It's a wonderful opportunity to catch up on news of all the 'family'.

It was at one of the Open Days that I met Sadie Twaddle and I told her about Mark. Sadie and her husband Alex had been part of a prayer support group for some time but had never been inside a prison. We quickly remedied that by inviting them to Dungavel the following day.

Questions poured forth from Mark as usual - but not for long! Alex was able to answer each one clearly and to Mark's satisfaction.

'Can you come back again next week?' he asked.

And so Alex, a youthful 78 year old, began his prison ministry.

Mark's questions were all finally answered and he asked Jesus to be his Saviour. After his release he enrolled in a Bible College. Alex still writes to him and prays for him.

Roy came to Dungavel from Saughton in 1983. He had been taken to see the film *The Cross and The Switchblade*. Roy had been brought up in a Christian home and married a lovely Christian wife, but he had never come to faith in Christ himself. Until he saw that film ...

He joined us in the Friday group and trusted Jesus as his Saviour and God for his future. On release in 1984 he started a Sunday School in Ferguslie. This led to work with people in need - especially alcoholics with nowhere to stay. He is now heavily involved in 'The Haven', a halfway house for those in need. 'Teen Challenge', founded by David Wilkerson who wrote *The Cross and the Switchblade* is taking responsibility for the venture. The story has come full circle!

James was one of the first inmates to make a personal commitment to Christ. We kept in touch with him when he was released and were glad to hear that he attended church regularly. He managed to find a job and even made a few friends of his own age.

In the past he had suffered from a family illness, but we thought it had all been resolved. Unfortunately the illness crept over him again. Although James was no longer in prison, the prison psychiatrist offered to see him and he was admitted to hospital. Ten years later he is still suffering but still telling other patients about the love Christ has for them - still sure of being with Christ one day. James is a special person to us. We continue to pray for his healing and try to visit or write to him regularly.

Hundreds of men have been acquainted or re-acquainted with the gospel of Jesus during our Fellowship meetings and there is not space to tell of them all, but you can read about Alan Fraser [see Chapter One] and John 'Rocky' Clark [see Chapter Five] as they tell their own stories.

Many have gone on strongly, set up halfway houses and used their own homes to reach others for Christ. Some are back as volunteers. Others speak to groups in and out of prison, telling of their lives, changed by the living Christ. God has indeed 'restored to them the years the locusts have eaten' as he promises in the Bible.

After Chuck's visit in 1981, he wrote to us saying: 'Keep up the faith. You're going to discover that there are many disappointments, frustrations and setbacks, but remember we are measured not by success but by faithfulness.' Those words were life-savers in the years which followed.

One evening we went to the prison to be greeted by the normally helpful and polite officers saying: 'So much for Christianity! One of your lads has been shipped' (meaning he had been returned to closed conditions). Our hearts sank until we remembered something else Chuck Colson had said: 'Considering the hostile reality of prison, the miracle is that so many do live for Christ behind bars, and then go on to make it on the outside. The more our ministry spreads, the more we see it happen. The gospel does change lives.'

But it is in God's timing, not ours! In the meantime we tried to remember that, when men are confined together, tempers flare. Sometimes violence is the only expression for them because so many have unresolved problems of normal communication.

During the early years we had the privilege of taking inmates to church with us. Imagine the shock for someone who had been 'inside' for ten years to be driven from the prison gates to a church service, with all the noise, the colour, the crowds!

One day we sat down to lunch with two astronauts who had been speaking at church and one of the prisoners remarked: 'Your head would be nothing like mine, coming from space to earth. I've had a more earth-shattering experience in church today than you'll ever have!' When prisoners were around, life was never dull!

Over the years we took inmates into our home for short and long stays. Tony Ralls, an ex-prisoner who provides aftercare for ex-prisoners, had warned about the cost of doing this.

In an article he wrote: 'We are talking about long-term commitment and high-cost investment without any promise of results ... There will be pain, as there is with physical ills; there will be demands; there will be a loss of sleep and a cost in time and emotional energy; but I believe that it is worth it!'

We found that there were times when the disruption to our household and lack of privacy caused problems, and we were tempted to put on a good face and hide our real feelings. The strain on family life was sometimes almost unbearable, but we survived the experience. The cost of keeping 'open house' has been great, but also rewarding and fulfilling.

We are so thankful for the many volunteers willing to join us faithfully on Friday evenings and for all who pray for us. And we remember more of Chuck Colson's words: 'We carry not a magic wand, but a Cross. And we must understand what the Cross signified - suffering, persecutions, seeming failures, not the success of the world but the ultimate and far greater reward of God's approval.'

As Lorraine mentioned, one member of her group at Dungavel is John 'Rocky' Clark. He can tell us stories from both sides, as you'll discover ...

> 'Therefore, if anyone is in Christ, he is a new
> creation; the old has gone, the new has come!
> All this is from God, who reconciled us to
> himself through Christ and gave us the ministry
> of reconciliation' (2 Corinthians 5:17-18).

5

CHANGING GANGS
by John 'Rocky' Clark,
Ex-inmate

I believe in miracles. Without them I should probably have committed suicide by now - or be in prison for murder.

I can't recall any contact with real Christianity in my childhood either at school or at home. But I do remember getting into trouble at a very early age. Even though I was terrified of my father's wrath, it never stopped me. I was stealing things by the time I was five, and had made a few court appearances before I was twelve. I was then handed over to the local authorities, and after a little while in a remand centre, I was taken to an orphanage in Banffshire.

I started drinking and trying out drugs when I was fourteen, but I preferred the drink. Two pals who started on drugs with me overdosed and died in their early twenties.

Although I had a job like most youngsters in the late sixties, I still did small-time break-ins into shops with a friend at weekends.

Not that I saw much good coming from the proceeds of crime. Once, I'd 'done a wee turn' and gone out the next day and bought new clothes. I looked really smart. That same night I did a 'smash and grab' at a licensed grocers. As soon as the large plate glass window was smashed, I moved quickly because the alarm was blaring away. I nearly got my head chopped off by a sheet of glass that came down like a guillotine. It cut my jacket, shirt and trousers and put a large gash on my shiny new shoes. Crime didn't pay that time!

It wasn't long before violence started creeping into things. I often got into fights and once I stabbed a guy, leaving him in a very serious condition. At that time I wouldn't have felt any remorse if he'd died - only fear of the consequences for me. Nothing I did had the power to move me.

The day after my sixteenth birthday I was sentenced to Borstal for house breaking. I was locked up again for most of the following year, 1971, in a Young Offenders' Institution - but that was my last charge for housebreaking. Pride made me feel it would be too embarrassing to be caught on such a charge again.

In 1972 I was sentenced to two years for police assault and serious assault. I'd stabbed a pub bouncer in the face with a beer glass and was lucky not to be sentenced to the High Court.

One incident happened during this sentence that was to have real significance in my life. I awoke one night to be confronted by the face of someone staring at me. I hadn't been near glue or alcohol and was wide awake.

I pulled the covers over my head and then thought I'd be brave by staring it out. When I looked out, the thing

53

smiled at me as if he knew exactly what I was thinking. My 'bottle' really crashed, because it was the most evil face you could imagine.

I shouted to my cell mate who was asleep, and the face disappeared. My cell mate must have believed in supernatural things because he was really frightened - or maybe he thought I might kill him in his sleep!

I went to see a minister the next morning and he told me to go away and pray. I thought this was a bit inadequate as I didn't really believe in God. But I went and prayed anyway and asked God - if he was there! - to take away this face and my fear of the devil.

For the first time in my life I knew there must be a God, because he did take away my fear. That night I slept like a baby and was never afraid of the devil again - as I often had been in the past. I don't really know who I saw that night, but I believe God allowed it to happen so that I would pray to him and learn that he was there and had power.

* * * * *

Over the next few years I was in many weekend fights, though I was never sent to jail. We had many 'carry-ons' with the family in my mother's house, all because of drink. We were a fairly sensible lot while sober, but it would be 'Murder...Polis' when we were in each other's company drinking! For instance, on the day I was married, my brother, who'd had 'just a few', threw an axe. It narrowly missed the pram that held my three-week-old baby son. Maybe this was my brother's way of saying 'Congratulations'!

Another incident happened one summer's night when I had something against a member of the family. It was so serious that I can't even remember what it was about! Anyway, I got hold of two petrol cans and went over to his house. Going round the back I found a window wide open.

I was just going to light the bomb and throw it when a voice very clearly said: 'That's the coward's way'. Pride surged inside me and I went round to the front garden. There I saw my brother's wife walking about in the living room. My brother was in a drunken sleep in a chair. I threw my lethal weapon at the window, but it bounced off and fell near my feet. I picked it up and threw it with as much force as I could, but to my horror it bounced back at great speed, hitting my leg and setting fire to my trousers. I hadn't realised it, but the windows in that area were reinforced plastic.

The following day I learned that two young children had been asleep in that back room, and I still thank the 'voice' which told me I was doing it the coward's way. It saved two children's lives.

Early in 1977 I got another two years for serious assault. By this time I was married and had two children. That sentence was very difficult for me especially when, after only a few months, I received bad news. I was shattered by it and for the next six months I tried to escape from reality into a dream world of my own. My dream was short and my mind played it back continually. It never bored me and even made me feel as if I were on drugs at times - which shows what the human mind is capable of! It was my way of getting out of prison, at least mentally, and it saved me from going bonkers.

It was during that time that I turned to God and prayed every day that he would protect the people I loved and sort out the huge mess I was in. Again, God did answer my prayers in a way which I feel would have been absolutely impossible without his intervention.

When I was released I went to England where my wife and two children were waiting. There I spent the happiest non-Christian year of my life. We both had jobs and even bought our own home, and I was drinking very little. We were very contented and glad to be away from the old life. I believed God had given us a real break.

But at New Year I had a call from my mother which made me homesick, and within weeks we were back in Kilmarnock. It was a grave mistake. Things got steadily worse from then on, and it wasn't long before I was back to 'normal'. Fighting, dishonesty and adultery became part and parcel of my life again.

During the next two years I was found 'not guilty' of three serious charges of assault. I stabbed a Doberman to death because it was supposed to have bitten someone I knew. A man with a shotgun came seeking revenge and laid siege to my house. My wife and the child she was holding in her arms, nearly got their heads blown off when they went too close to a window.

Another pub fight earned me three years for serious assault, but I was released on bail on Christmas Eve 1982. I had just spent three and a half months awaiting trial and felt the need to be home for Christmas - hence the bail. But it was a big mistake.

Deep down, I knew that God wanted me to stay inside for Christmas, and I told my wife so. But I disobeyed that inner voice - I did go out on bail, and for the next seven months it was all downhill. It ended with my being charged with attempted murder which landed me back inside. Even if I got away with it, I'd still have to finish my three years.

This time I knew I had really blown it and messed up completely. The only thing I valued in life was my family, but once again, I'd left my wife pregnant, with four young children around her feet, breaking her heart. I hadn't always been kind to her, but she was still the only person I cared about. She was all I had. What a fool I was!

But God hadn't washed his hands of me. Even though my mind was in a turmoil, I heard God's voice asking me to plead guilty to my outstanding charge. It was the last thing I wanted to do! But in the long mental battle that followed, his voice continued to speak even louder: 'Plead guilty'.

I told my wife about it, but she was against the idea.

'That's all I need,' she said, 'you to throw away more years of our lives!'

I turned to the Bible to see if I could find a verse that would say I didn't need to plead guilty, even though I *was* guilty. Naturally I never found one.

That night I started writing a letter to my wife about how this was to be my last time in jail, and what a good life we'd have next time round. But I knew I was kidding myself. And suddenly I just laid my pen down and started to cry. It wasn't just ordinary crying. The tears were literally like heavy raindrops, flooding down on to the floor and I was completely powerless to halt them.

And I didn't even want to stop them. These tears were for all that had happened in the past - for the wee boy who had been sent away from his family; for the young man

57

in the institutions and jail; for all the bad things I'd done; for the unloving way I'd treated my wife and children; for the man I now was - alone and deeply lonely. I cried for all the love I had never received and for the fears I'd lived with for years.

In that moment I was truly sorry for my whole sordid life. I told God I would plead guilty at court for him, and only asked that he would change me before I was ever let out again. Otherwise I knew I'd waste the rest of my life, no matter how good my intentions were.

It is hard to describe the lovely sense of peace which came flowing over me that night. All my anxiety disappeared and I knew somehow that my life was going to be okay from then on.

The next day I asked to see a chaplain (I'd only ever spoken to one chaplain before and that was ten years previously). This man approached me at recreation, which was rather embarrassing as lots of 'cons' were standing around. But he gave me a wee book called *Our Daily Bread* and a Christian newspaper called *Challenge*.

That night in my cell I discovered, through these small Christian booklets and the Bible, that Jesus Christ was the way to be put right with God. I think that was the first time I'd heard about salvation. I'd imagined that I was right with God because I was going to plead guilty!

I continued to read about Jesus, and it seemed that no matter where I looked in the Bible, Jesus was there. Fascinated, I read for almost four days about how he had died for my sins and that by accepting his atonement I would find forgiveness and be on right terms with God. And that's exactly what I did. I knelt down and asked

Jesus to come into my heart and forgive my sins.

From then on I was right with God and had been 'born again' by his Spirit into new life. The Bible says that 'if anyone is in Christ, he is a new creation'. Well, that's just how I felt. I started praying to God and Jesus in quite a new way.

The most wonderful thing about those first few weeks was the love and closeness I felt to Jesus and God. He showered me with a feeling of absolute serenity. With my heart swept clean of all the filth and sin, I wanted to show God's love to my wife and others around me, but most of all to God. The Bible says that 'we love him because he first loved us'. How true I found this.

One day my lawyer and his young assistant came to see me. I explained that I was now a Christian and therefore couldn't tell lies in the witness box. I don't know if this is what he wanted to hear, but his young assistant seemed to be very pleased for me, judging by the delighted look on his face. This encouraged me - not for my sake, but for his. As I walked away, I felt absolutely tremendous.

I went to court and signed the section admitting all. On the way back to the cells I was allowed a moment's conversation with my wife. It had been raining and she was soaked through. Her hair was a mess and her face looked thin and tired. She had only just had our fifth child and an operation - she probably looked at her worst.

But the amazing thing was that I spent the rest of that day waiting to go back to Barlinnie, with thoughts of the beautiful woman I had just seen. I couldn't get over how pure and lovely she looked.

I lost my appeal and was sent back to Barlinnie to

serve three years. I soon met Alfred Bowie, the hall Chaplain, and he proved to be a real 'godsend', someone I could talk to about spiritual things. Alf was a true 'born again' believer and knew just how to encourage me. He would come into my work place for a chat, and I wasn't in the least embarrassed now, even if there were four or five 'Killie' guys sitting around. I spent a fair bit of time telling these men what had just happened in my life - in fact, I told anyone who would listen.

Alf introduced me to Prison Fellowship on Thursday night and the Bible class on Sunday afternoon. It was the first time I knew such things existed in prisons. I started to get uptight on Thursday nights in case my door wasn't opened for the Prison Fellowship meeting.

It was quite formal and consisted mainly of Bible Study, but I was extremely eager to learn. The Sunday group was very different in that it was lively, musical and had an evangelistic gospel message. Together they provided a proper balance for me.

A few months later when I was moved to Perth, I felt really sad to leave Barlinnie, where I first learned all that Jesus had done for me.

I spent the next year or so in Perth prison and I enjoyed both the Prison Fellowship group on Monday evenings and the Bible Class on Sunday afternoon. It was at the Sunday group that I came to know a Christian couple from my home town of Kilmarnock and through these people, my wife and children started to attend church and Sunday School. I was delighted that they were hearing about Jesus from somebody other than myself!

But my wife did not go there lightly. At that point she resented and feared any kind of intrusion into her life. She also had her 'time' to do, and people coming close to her shook her wee bit of 'security'. If I hadn't been a Christian, no other Christian would have got their foot inside our door. My wife hated what she thought of as 'interfering people'.

In Perth I spent a lot of time learning from the Bible. I hardly ever went to recreation because it seemed a waste of time. My mind was too occupied with reading Christian books and writing to have any spare time. I liked nothing better than to come in from work and close the door of my cell until the next morning.

But I did look forward to the Fellowship classes, though I longed to talk more about what was happening in my life. Unfortunately there is very little time for one-to-one conversation in prison. I missed the talks I'd had with Alf Bowie in Barlinnie so I was grateful to God when another Christian 'con' arrived, and we were able to help each other to grow in our faith as we discussed the meaning of Bible verses.

I moved to Dungavel for the rest of my sentence. At first I found conditions very trying. It seemed that you couldn't blink an eye without it being noticed! There was no shutting one's cell door here! It was all small dormitories, and I soon found that my patience and tolerance were going to be severely tested.

If Perth had been a cosy, growing period, this was anything but! I attended both Prison Fellowship groups at Dungavel - one on Wednesday and the other on Friday nights. The latter was run by Duncan and Lorraine Ferguson and Pat McCracken. Their obvious love for God made for a good atmosphere in the groups. I looked forward to the Bible studies and testimonies and just generally being with people of my own kind for fellowship. I found a place of contentment with the Christians there because of their balance between strong fundamental beliefs and the way they gave young Christians space to grow.

I had many opportunities at Dungavel to speak to the other 'cons' about having Jesus in my life - and I suppose they had the chance to see how it was working out. I found very few who wouldn't converse with me, despite my coolness to wrongdoing within the prison system. Sometimes I was able to have one-to-one conversations with non-Christian inmates and pray with them about their problems. Sometimes I was asked to pray for the 'asker', an inmate who was too shy to pray for himself, but who saw some kind of hope in 'my' God.

Some prisoners maintain that one can't be a Christian 'inside' because the temptations and trials of living with other prisoners are too great. I have been on both sides of the prison wall as a Christian and I think it is harder to stand on the 'outside'. The pressures of ordinary living are so much greater, especially for family men, who have a huge responsibility as head of their home. Married or single, inside or out, I believe that most of our problems come from our own heart.

When I was finally released from Dungavel I felt really sad to be leaving the Fellowship group. I was even sad for all the prisoners I was leaving behind. God had changed my 'heart of stone' and I felt full of compassion for them all. The day I left, the Lord told me in three different ways that one day I would be going back to take his message to them. I knew then that at least part of my future was going to be back in prisons.

On my release I joined a church immediately. This

was largely due to Harry Hunter, who had been visiting me in prison. My wife had become a Christian eight months after me, and she and the children were already attending that church and Sunday School. So not only was I going out to a new church, but to a 'new' wife. It was indeed a blessing to our marriage.

I found the Christians at Elim Hall, Kilmarnock, very open in their acceptance of me. Although I took this for granted at the time, I realise now that I was very fortunate in this respect. I had my ups and downs within the church and caused many problems for some believers, but I was baptised there and stayed in fellowship for some time. I have moved now, but I still pop in occasionally and enjoy speaking to Christian friends.

I also discovered that God doesn't just care for spiritual needs - he helped me in material ways too. It was several months before I found a paying job and money was tight. But just when a bill was needing to be paid, or we needed something we couldn't afford, we received a letter with a wee cheque from Christians we hardly even knew - not a lot, but sufficient to see us through. It was really humbling to find that God cared even about a small electricity bill.

For the last six years I have worked as a self-employed painter and I believe that God has given me every single job, because he cares about all aspects of our lives.

I didn't have any trouble with old enemies when I got out of jail. Everyone knew I wasn't into fighting any more - and I have to admit that it was usually me who started the fights anyway! My relatives accepted that I'd had some kind of religious experience and was maybe 'over the top' a bit. Fortunately, my ways are a bit different from theirs nowadays, but unfortunately this has put up its own kind of barrier.

In my own family, my twelve-year-old daughter gave her life to Christ not long after I got out. My other children are well aware of the gospel and I thank Elim Hall Sunday School for this. I sometimes think, if God hadn't changed me, what kind of home would they have grown up in?

After I had been out of prison for a time, Duncan and Lorraine Ferguson asked me to come back into Dungavel with them. I am now part of the Prison Fellowship team and I sit where I used to sit as a 'con'. I have also visited other prisons with the Prison Fellowship volunteers, trying to show how God can change even the hardest people.

My hope is that God will use my life experiences to help others make room in their lives for Christ. He is a great leader, and the best thing I ever did was to join his gang.

* * * * *

Eddie Murison is another 'tough guy' who changed gangs. He too is now a Prison Fellowship volunteer in Aberdeen, where his story starts ...

> 'He upholds the cause of the oppressed and
> gives food to the hungry. The LORD sets
> prisoners free' (Psalm 146:7).

6

HOOKED BY LOVE
by Eddie 'Eddie Boy' Murison,
Ex-inmate

A reject and a rebel - that was me from the age of four, when I first realised that my stepfather didn't want me. I think he was jealous of my relationship with my mother, and he abused me verbally and physically.

So I rebelled - both at home and at school. Once, when my teacher attempted to correct my behaviour and attitude, I broke into the classroom and had a bonfire with the textbooks. But when the blaze was going I got scared, and smothered it with foam from the fire extinguishers, leaving my footprints as evidence. It was my first crime - I was nine years old.

Around the same time I started to run away from home. One day, when we were living in Banff, which is about forty miles north of Aberdeen, I jumped on an old bike and headed for the city. I got as far as Inverurie when the police stopped me and took me back home. After that I ran away frequently, so it was agreed that I could go and stay with my grandfather in Aberdeen and go to school there.

By the time I was fourteen I had been involved in a lot

of crimes: breaking into cars for joy rides; taking what was in the car; breaking into shops for money and drink.

'This is the life for me,' I thought. 'I'll get what I want without asking. I'll just take it.'

Of course I got caught. Because I was only fourteen I was sent for two years to a List D Approved School at Rossie Farm, Montrose. There I used to steal food and hide it, and then I would run back to Aberdeen for two or three months before I was caught again.

While on the run, I lived by breaking into places for food, money, clothes and drink. Stealing was becoming a way of life. So was drink. I started to need a drink every day. I would spend all the money I had on drink, and if I didn't have money to buy it, I would steal to get some. I was well on the road to becoming a habitual criminal and getting deeper into it day by day.

I carried on stealing and fighting, and was sent to Borstal. After that I was sent to a Young Offenders' Institution and then to prison. It was the end of the line. I was a 'con'. This looked like the way it would be for the rest of my life.

The next years saw me in and out of prison. I was also into my second marriage. I remember walking home one night. I knew the police were looking for me, and for some reason I looked up at the sky and shouted: 'If there is a God, let me have this night with my wife and daughter before the police pick me up.'

The police came the next morning! That time I was in remand for three months, and then sentenced to two and a half years. Even in prison I got into trouble for fighting and smashing things so I was moved from Edinburgh to Dumfries prison to finish my time.

It was in Dumfries prison that I received a 'Dear John' letter from my wife. It was handed to me on Christmas Day by a prison officer with a smile on his face. Anger boiled inside me - partly against my wife, but against the prison officer even more.

My anger set me against everybody and I was just looking for trouble. I knew that one of the prison officers there drank a lot so I decided to 'do' him so I could get his drink. But every time I went for him, there would be another prison officer around.

I attacked a 'con' who was walking past me, just because I heard from his accent that he was English - like my wife! I ended up in detention where I fought with the three prison officers who came to take my clothes.

After a week or two in the detention cell the Chaplain, Bill McKenzie, came to see me. He said that God had sent him to help me.

'This is a joke,' I thought, and I told him so.

'God loves you,' he said. He went away then, but left behind a leaflet called *Journey Into Life*. I couldn't really read or write as I had never attended school for any length of time, so I had never read any books. I thought about what he'd said, picked up the leaflet, then threw it down again.

Later that day I picked up a book called *Hooked* by Ernie Hollands, an ex-prisoner. For the first time in my life I read a book right through. Then I got the leaflet and read it through. I didn't know it at the time, but God was showing me how to read!

At six o'clock that Friday night I asked Jesus Christ to come into my life. For the first time in my whole life I felt good, really good. I knew God had started something good in me.

My attitude towards 'cons' and prison officers changed for the better. I felt that, because I was a Christian, I had to start being good towards other people. For the first time ever, I began to accept the system instead of fighting it.

In the ten months that followed there was trouble in prisons all over Scotland, with many riots. The Dumfries 'cons' were moved to other prisons. All the other Christian 'cons' in Dumfries were moved to Shotts Prison, but I was sent to Glenochil Prison.

I felt out on a limb. I was scared I might forget my faith. I had only two or three months left to go and moving to a new prison was not easy. I thought I might have to prove myself again, but the Prison Fellowship group in that prison supported me and helped me keep hold of my faith.

One day my life was in danger. Four guys were all 'tooled up' and out to get me. I had only weeks left to serve, and I remember saying to the Prison Fellowship couple, Frankie and Eddie Macguire: 'If you really believe in God, pray that nothing happens to me.'

The next day I walked over to one of the guys and took his knife from him. 'God doesn't want you to do this,' I said.

The four guys ended up in my cell and I found myself speaking about the love of God and what he could do for them. We met a few times in my cell after that and talked about Christ and what he was doing in my life. The Bible says, 'If God is for us, who can be against us?'

On 12th October, 1987, I was released from prison and went to stay with Eddie and Frankie Macguire from Prison Fellowship. I knew they understood the new life I had started with God and I knew they would be able to help me.

While staying with them I went through a deep

spiritual experience. I felt my old life being washed away and I was filled with a new life. I had heard this could happen, but it was wonderful to experience it for myself.

Later I returned to Aberdeen to live. I found a good church, which I still attend. At first I found it hard to mix with people. I thought they were all snobs, but thanks to the people in Prison Fellowship, I have gradually started to open up more as a person. God used Prison Fellowship to help me get rid of some of my old hurts and learn to trust people for the first time in my life.

One day at church I felt God asking me to help feed the homeless in Aberdeen, so I started to walk the streets at night with blankets and flasks of soup. I wanted to give people something warm to drink and cover themselves with. This went on for about six months and then I was allowed to use the church building as a base.

At first only five or six people came in during the day, but it grew. We called it OFTAN - Outreach For the Aberdeen Needy. Homeless people came in first thing in the morning. They could take a shower, have breakfast and lunch and even get a change of clothes from a stock which had been donated. They could also return later for something hot before sleeping on the streets.

At lunchtimes, once the meal was over, I used to talk about Jesus and the Bible and what God could do for them, if only they would let him. I've seen really hard men in tears as God reached out to them. It is beautiful to see the changes that come upon people's lives when God touches them.

One day a drunken man started shouting that I was a 'con man' and that he hated me. He was shouting and swearing, and then he came up and threw a punch at me, right on the chest. I didn't feel a thing! I remember putting my hand on his head and praying for him. He went flat on his face in front of everybody and he got up stone cold sober a few minutes later. He said he had seen Christ in my face and wanted to find him in his own life.

Another day my partner, Don, and I prayed for food to feed the people who would be coming in that day. Two hours later a van came from Peterhead with six hundred cans of soup for us! God was answering prayer as we reached out to help others.

During this time I married a Christian girl. She was definitely the right girl for me. We both go to the Prison Fellowship Group in Aberdeen. Through Prison Fellowship I have visited Glenochil prison, talking to the men there too. I even knew some of the guys in prison! My wife and I both feel that God is moving us into this kind of work and we love to do it.

After all the troubles in my earlier life, the hardest fight for me was to stay a Christian once I got outside. All the temptations were just looking at me wherever I went. I am learning to trust myself to stand by my commitment to God and to trust other people to help me to get through my change of personality. It's a hard struggle sometimes.

When I look back, I see God's hand in my life and how he used Prison Fellowship to pull me out of the wasted life I was in. God had plans for me. He reached out to me when I thought I would not be good enough to be a Christian. He showed me how to put my old life behind me and go for the new life he had planned for me.

On 14th January, 1993 I will have been a Christian for six years, and God is still standing by me and doing great things in my life. He helped me to get a job with British

Rail where I have now been promoted to being a Leading Trackman.

It hasn't all been straight going though. About six months after my release, I fell flat on my face with drink. I had got drunk and ended up in a fight and really hurt a guy. That night I went on my knees in prayer before God and asked him to help me to stop drinking and doing crazy things. Then I opened my Bible and read some words in Isaiah 51:22. I knew God meant them for me. 'This is what your Sovereign LORD says, your God, who defends his people: "See, I have taken out of your hand the cup that made you stagger; from that cup ... you will never drink again." ' I have never taken alcohol since that day.

Prayer is the way I ask God for help, and he has never let me down. I know I've come a long, hard road, but Jesus has given me the best life. He carries me at times when I feel I can't keep going. In prison I had given up, but then God came in and showed me the way out of Hell. Prison was Hell to me, but through the Chaplain and Prison Fellowship, God renewed my mind and set me free. He still comes this way for guys like me, if they will just realise that Christ is the only way out - if we are to stay 'out'.

* * * * *

Crucial people in Eddie's life were the Macguires. Frankie tells how she and her husband became involved in Prison Fellowship in the next chapter....

> 'Is not this the kind of fasting I have chosen: to loose the chains of injustice ... to set the oppressed free and break every yoke? Is it not to share your food with the hungry and to provide the poor wanderer with shelter - when you see the naked to clothe him ... Then your light will break forth like the dawn and your healing will quickly appear ... you will be called Repairer of Broken Walls'
>
> (Isaiah 58: 6-12).

7

REPAIRERS OF BROKEN WALLS
by Frances 'Frankie' Macguire
Prison Fellowship, H.M. Prison, Glenochil

If you were looking for an example of an average family, we Macguires would have been it. Eddie was an ambitious sales representative. I was a mother with two young daughters. We lived in a pleasant house in a small rural town. I had always been a churchgoer. Eddie also attended regularly - once a year on Christmas Eve!

In 1980 everything changed. God began to make his presence felt. I realised that, although I knew all about God, I didn't know him as a person. Then I learned that, in order to get to know him, I would have to let go of my pride and my 'religiousness' and come to him like a little child. After many sleepless nights and troubled days I finally surrendered.

Eddie was pleased for me. He saw that somehow I was

overcoming all the irrational fears that had gripped my life until then. I had been terrified of illness, of dying, of being alone in the house for fear someone would break in, afraid to go out at night, afraid of something happening to the children. It was a great relief to Eddie to see the difference my new faith made.

Later on that year he decided to go along to a communicants' class with a view to joining the church. He thought it would be a good way of becoming part of the local community. But he hadn't reckoned on meeting God!

For several months he wrestled with the fact that, if God really existed and Jesus really came into the world to die in order that we might have a way back to God, then he had to make a response. Finally he did give in and the Macguire family embarked on a new life that was to break the mould of anything we had known before.

About three years after we had become Christians we admitted to each other that we felt God had something specific for us to do. We didn't really know exactly what it was - we just sensed something in our spirits. Reading the Bible separately, we had both been struck by words in Isaiah 58, and we felt that somehow we were meant to reach out to the 'poor and needy' mentioned in that chapter. But who were they?

At first we naturally thought of people who were materially poor. Later on we realised that, without Jesus, everybody is in the 'poor' category.

Circumstances seemed to show that our 'poor and needy' were alcoholics, drug addicts and down-and-outs. In our naivety we started looking for a large house in which we could 'minister' to these people. After many disappointments we learned that God didn't want what little strengths we had, or our abilities, or even our enthusiasm. He just wanted us to surrender our lives and hand the controls to him.

In 1985 we attended a Christian Coffee Club meeting to hear Louise Purvis speak about Prison Fellowship. We had heard Chuck Colson some years before but, although it had been interesting, we had no desire whatsoever to go near a prison. We did feel, however, that a link with Prison Fellowship might be useful as it was possible we would consider taking ex-prisoners into our 'retreat' house.

After the meeting we were introduced to the Assistant Prison Governor of our local prison, Glenochil Young Offenders' Institution. He had recently become a Christian and, after attending a Prison Fellowship weekend some months before, he had started a Prison Fellowship group in Glenochil. Louise asked us if we would be prepared to form a prayer group to pray for them. We agreed to an initial prayer meeting and arranged a date.

The first prayer meeting included a prison governor, a social worker, a prison officer and a prison visitor. We were surrounded by experts! But there is nothing like first-hand experience, so it was suggested that we go into the prison the following Sunday to meet the members of the Prison Fellowship group.

When we walked into the prison chapel that first Sunday, we knew with an inexplicable certainty that we were in the place where God meant us to be. We had no experience, no training, no confidence. But we somehow felt the love that God had for these men. We had intended to make a 'one off' visit to meet the young men we were praying for, but we have been going into Glenochil almost every Sunday since!

It is important to remember that at the outset we had no desire to get involved in prison work. We had wanted to keep it at arm's length. Like most of the general public, we regarded prisoners as a different species who perhaps warranted some pity, but mostly were in need of correction and reform. To our great surprise we met real people - just like us!

It was an unnerving experience, but a thrilling one too. We were able to relate as equals, sharing the same inner struggles, reaching out towards God who was always there, and discovering that, in Christ there really are no barriers of background, age, sex, colour or denomination.

One particular event stands out in that first year. The occasion was a Prison Fellowship weekend. It had been an exciting time, with a concert on the Friday night and testimonies and discussion groups on the Saturday. It culminated in a service in the gymnasium on Sunday morning, with about a hundred inmates attending. As the service progressed the presence of the Holy Spirit was almost tangible. Many hardened and cynical young men broke down in tears, and we believe they will never forget that experience.

The theme of the weekend was 'Hope for the Future', and one of the young men present was Peter. He was twenty years old and just starting a life sentence.

'What hope have I got?' he asked. 'What future?'

But God reached down through the black, gaping horror of the years ahead and gave Peter new birth into a living hope, a new life filled with love, joy, peace and so much more. It was as if a light had been switched on inside Peter. He has moved on from Glenochil now, and

God has done amazing things through him, as you will read in the following chapter.

We continued to look for our 'retreat house' and in fact were offered the tenancy of a suitable property. So far advanced were our plans that we had offered a place in the house to a young man who was about to be released from Glenochil.

In order to finalise the arrangements for the house, the whole family went to stay for the weekend. By this time we had learnt to depend more on God's promptings than on our own reasoning and, although the house seemed to be the answer to our prayers, both Eddie and I were conscious of a deep disquiet over the whole arrangement. So we shared our feelings with the owner and amicably pulled out of the agreement, with no ill feelings and a large helping of grace on the part of the owner!

But we were left with the problem of Willie, our first resident-to-be, who was due for release in a matter of weeks. There was nothing else for it but to offer to have him to stay in our own home.

When we both gave our lives to God originally, we had been challenged by the fact that our family of three daughters was a 'god' to us, and that we had to be willing to allow God to be our number one priority and entrust our girls to his care. This is all very well in theory - but now we were going to have to put it into practice!

We converted our dining room into a bed-sitting room and prepared to have our first resident. We picked Willie up from the gates of Glenochil at 7.00 a.m. on a fine summer's morning, and a new phase of our journey had begun.

We spent an eventful few weeks with Willie. Our

lifestyles were completely different. He slept half the day and watched television all night. It was difficult to sort out what was really important to God and what was just 'culture'. But we made some progress, and it was a learning process for us all.

Then one day Willie disappeared. He had gone back to his old familiar lifestyle and was back in prison within ten days.

From that experience, and with the next few men who came to stay, we learned that, unless a man is following Jesus for himself, you can pour out all you have and it will just be consumed to no real purpose, though God, in his grace, may 'sow a few seeds' along the way.

Only God has the power to break the hold of pride and self in a life, but he will only do that if the person is willing. He will never invade a life where he is not welcome. Someone told a story about the Prodigal Son, saying that if Christians had come along and given him fish suppers when he was working with the pigs, he would never have gone back to his father! Sadly, by intervening and propping up a life, we can sometimes be perpetuating a wrong situation and preventing that person from seeing his need of God and turning to him in a life-changing way.

We must depend on the Holy Spirit to know when to help and when to stand back. We cannot trust our natural compassion. Jesus did not always rush to people. He moved only at his Father's prompting. Many people, particularly women, get involved in prison work, moved by natural compassion rather than by the Spirit of God. Often they get hurt, disappointed and bitter, feeling: 'After all I've done, this is what I get!' Jesus has little sympathy for such an attitude. We need to depend on God, not gratitude, for our fulfilment.

The Christian life is demanding and exciting, but never boring or predictable. So it should have been no surprise when, after about a year of leading Prison Fellowship groups in Glenochil, there was a massive upheaval.

The Young Offenders' Institution was changed into an adult high security prison. We were not sure how we would cope with big-time, grown-up criminals and had to trust that God would equip us. We found, of course, as with the Young Offenders, the adults were real, ordinary people like ourselves.

The transition was made easier when one of the Young Offenders returned to Glenochil to complete his sentence. He had been a stalwart in our group but had been transferred to an adult prison when he became twenty-one. It meant a lot to us to have a familiar face at the meeting, especially as he was eager to know more of God.

At that stage we only had three or four men coming along on a Sunday, but we developed a closeness and a trusting openness which is seldom found in prison. Prisoners tend to trust no-one and live behind a barrier of their own making, for their own protection. Often invited speakers at the meetings are disappointed by the lack of response to their message. Very often this is because the inmates have trained themselves not to respond, not to show reactions or emotions. However, it doesn't mean that nothing is happening inside beneath the stony exteriors.

At home we had our first adult ex-prisoner staying

with us, and what a blessing that was to us all! Jim had a serious drug habit, but had been set free by the power of God.

The first night he was with us he volunteered to wash the dishes. When he accidentally cut his finger on a sharp knife, he ran into the bathroom, where we found him pale-faced and shaking. I offered him a sticking plaster but he pushed me away. Then we realised that Jim was HIV positive. He had only recently found out himself.

We praised God for the way it had happened because the Aids panic was rife at that time, and had we known beforehand we might not have let him come to stay. We would have been paralysed with fear. But the phrase, 'Do not be afraid', appears hundreds of times in the Bible. If we trust God, we need not be afraid.

We took normal hygiene measures with Jim, and the Lord even sent along a doctor, who specialised in dealing with Aids sufferers, to reassure us.

Jim told us that in the past, as soon as he walked through the prison gates all he could think of was where he could get a 'fix'. This time it had been different - there was no craving, only peace, and a tingling anticipation of what God had in store. He spent his time with us enjoying the presence of God and the countryside, while God repaired his body and his mind.

After a few weeks he decided to visit his family and his girlfriend. He was so confident of his new-found strength. He phoned to say he was staying over and that his girlfriend was coming off drugs and had made a commitment to Christ. But he came back unsettled and jangled the following day.

Jim desperately wanted to share his faith with his

friends who were caught up in the meaningless drug culture. He eventually went back to the city, full of high hopes, but we ached inside for him. It takes time for full healing to take place and for strength to be built up. Out of human compassion, Jim moved out too soon and within weeks was sucked back into the drug scene. We only ever saw him once again - a gaunt shell, forever on the move, responding to regular knocks on the door.

In our experience, very few people 'make it' when they go straight back to where they came from. Those who do, have really active, understanding churches or Christian wives and families to support them.

In Glenochil our numbers were increasing and many who came along were looking for something real to replace all that was false and meaningless in their lives. At the same time they were afraid of being let down again. Fear is one of the devil's greatest weapons. We noticed that all the people who stayed with us had an escape route planned, so that when the time came to face up to the thing they were afraid of, they could run away rather than confront the issue. We can say categorically that everyone who has been enabled to stay and face the problem has come through victoriously in the power of God. We have seen him deliver people when we had no faith left to believe it was possible.

As we became more involved with ex-prisoners, God began to draw our attention to some practical needs. Men often leave prison with only the clothes they went in with, a small discharge grant and a travel warrant for home. Many have been divorced whilst in prison and are therefore released to start afresh, alone and lonely. The prospect of setting up home from scratch is just too much for them to cope with. They are very vulnerable at that point and often enter into unfortunate relationships rather than try to cope with the mountainous problems of making it on their own. Many cannot manage their money - or don't have enough money to manage - and they return to crime to pay mounting debts.

We wondered if it would be possible to supply some furniture and clothing to help them through the initial period and, through church magazines and local Christian bookshops, we appealed for these things. We were given the use of an old warehouse and worked one day a week with Community Service for Offenders. They provided a suitable vehicle and two men, who were serving Community Service orders, to help with the physical work. It was amazing how people responded. God knows every need and we never lacked anything that was required.

We now run two groups in the prison: an outreach meeting on Sunday afternoons and a Bible class on Wednesday evenings. On Sundays we encourage the men to bring their friends along to a relaxed meeting where we usually have a visiting speaker. Visitors with musical ministries are very popular and they often leave tapes and give us permission to copy and distribute them to all who want them. Most of the men have facilities available for listening to taped music, and we have found that the Lord often touches people at a very deep level through music and songs.

Not long ago one of the men who had stayed with us on his release from prison came to one of our Prison Fellowship meetings. Eddie Murison spoke most convincingly about the transforming power of God in his life.

Strangely enough one of the men present that night recognised Eddie from some years back on the 'outside'. He had heard about Eddie's conversion but had reckoned there must been a 'con' in it somewhere. Eddie also recognised the inmate from his bad old days. Indeed he had once spent eighteen months searching for him to settle an old score. Now that he had found him the desire for revenge, the fear and the violence were all gone. The two men shook hands warmly, reconciled and forgiven.

When we get these fleeting glimpses of what God is doing they are like rainbows - a sign of God and his love, beyond our comprehension, but there none the less.

We saw such a glimpse in Kenny. He couldn't read or write but he came along one Wednesday night as we were starting a study of Luke's Gospel. When the time came for us to finish, he was desperate to read on. We had to go but the following week he told us that he had taken the little Gospel with him and had read it from beginning to end. God still works miracles!

He works miracles in men in prison who are often despised by the world, but never by God. He does not overlook their sin, but through Jesus he reaches past the sin to bring healing and forgiveness to all who come to him in childlike trust. He builds strong, new lives that are fulfilled, exciting and satisfying. He is the ultimate in human restoration - 'the Repairer of broken walls.'

* * * * *

Frankie mentioned Peter Kelly. Right now he is serving a life sentence in Saughton Prison. Read on to find out why....

> 'Return to your fortress, O prisoners of hope:
> even now I announce that I will restore twice as
> much to you' (Zechariah 9:12)

8

BREAKING THROUGH THE BARRIERS
by Peter Kelly,
Inmate

The word 'murderer' conjures up many images to those
who hear it.

Did I fit one of those images? Do I now? Through
most of my life I was a broken person. I don't say that to
justify any of my actions, but it is important that I tell you
about some of that brokenness which, in its own way,
moulded my life. Only then will the healing power of the
Lord Jesus Christ be seen.

My earliest memories are of my father, whom I loved.
Unfortunately he died when I was three and a half years
old. It was as if my world had crashed, especially when
I was sent to live with an aunt in Ireland until my mother
could come to grips with the hole which his death had
created in her life.

I needed my mother. No matter how much my relatives tried to make me one of the family, it was never the
same. All my memories of that time are bad ones. I was
too young to be able to take in the fuller picture, so I put
two and two together and came up with the belief that I
was unloved and unwanted. From that time on I began to

erect emotional barriers, and I was determined to stay behind them.

In the end I was re-united with my mother and brothers, but by that time it was too late. I no longer felt like a son or a brother, but like a complete stranger. I became more introverted, and this was evident at school. I can never remember a time when I didn't feel inferior to those around me. It just always seemed to be that way. So I kept my mask firmly in place.

When I was nine I was sexually abused by a boy five or six years older than myself. It was one more nail in my emotional coffin. No matter how many times I washed myself, I still felt soiled and dirty. How could I share that with anyone? All I could do was bottle it up inside and erect more barriers. In a sad way it confirmed how worthless I felt I was.

If I had been withdrawn before, I became even more so. I really just closed up inside. No matter who I was with, be it friends or family, I always felt as if I was 'with' but never really 'part' of them. This caused enormous problems at school. I did have my fair share of pals, but it was all very superficial.

With hindsight I realise that no-one ever got really close to me in those days. Barriers not only lock others out, they lock you in, and once I was locked in, I just didn't know how to get back out again.

At secondary school I was a regular truanter. I just couldn't cope with the isolation I felt, being surrounded by so many people, but never belonging. At least when I was alone I had no obligations and could do what I wanted when I wanted.

When the School Board lady came to our house, as she

regularly did because I was so often absent from school, I just shrugged my shoulders and promised to go back. How could I tell her - or anybody - what I really felt like inside? Where would I start - and who would listen even if I could? I loved my mother and brothers but could never begin to open up to them and say what I really felt like. I felt there was just no-one I could turn to.

At the age of fourteen I was abused again. This was the last straw emotionally. It destroyed any understanding of what relationships with anyone should be. Sexually and emotionally it created total havoc within my life. I didn't feel I could relate to anyone - I felt totally worthless and useless.

I found my escape in gambling. It was an addiction that stayed with me for years, both while I was in prison and even after I became a Christian. I could write pages telling about what I did to get money to satisfy my habit. It got to the stage that no-one trusted me, and this only reinforced my brokenness.

Gambling became my crutch, my escape from the reality I couldn't cope with. And it succeeded in destroying any remaining good that others may have seen in me. With every broken trust, another part of me died inside.

I had many chances and many people bent over backwards to help me. But the problem was inside me, and I found no one I would have allowed to help deal with it.

Due to gambling, I got into trouble and carried a knife. On one of the nights that I was carrying a knife, I got involved in a pub fight. The result was the death of a young man. He took the full force of years of bottled up emotions. A few hours later I handed myself in to the police and in due course, I went through the judicial system.

Words will never be able to express my feelings about his needless death and the pain caused to his family and friends. To say 'Sorry' is totally inadequate.

I began to pray a lot - not for myself, but for the family of the man I had killed, for my own family, and that God's will would be done. By the time I went back to court for the verdict I had peace in my heart. I received a life sentence.

I started my sentence at Glenochil as a Young Offender. There I started attending Prison Fellowship meetings. This helped my vague relationship with God to develop and grow, and my understanding of him became clearer. I began to comprehend that the Lord had his hand upon me. There was a real yearning in my spirit, though I didn't know what that yearning was for. God had been the only one I ever turned to in bad times, but I found myself turning to him more and more in everyday situations.

All this came to a climax in 1986 at a 'Fellowship weekend' run by Prison Fellowship and the Chaplains. During the weekend, a few more pieces of the jigsaw started to fit together. I began to see my responsibility to God more clearly. But more importantly, I began to grasp how, by sending Jesus, God was reaching out to the whole world, and even to me!

When an ex-prisoner speaker called Jim asked us to make a decision for Jesus, I really felt I had no choice but to give my life to him. It was the start of a new way of life, one which has brought both change and healing.

I asked if Prison Fellowship could allocate me a

visitor and soon afterwards Eddie, one of the Prison Fellowship leaders at Glenochil, came to see me. He brought his wife, Frankie, with him. I cannot adequately express the help these two people gave me and I thank God for them.

One day the Lord said that if I wanted to be fully healed, I must totally open my heart and share my brokenness with this couple. 'No way, Lord.' I said. 'Don't even think of asking such a thing!'

The truth was that I knew there were many areas in my life that I just couldn't face myself, and there was certainly no way I was prepared to share them with others.

But I soon discovered that the gentle love of the Lord is hard to resist, and eventually I had to submit. With much fear I opened up to them. I'd like to say I felt good about it right away, but all I could think of when I'd done it was: 'Oh no! What have I done?' But their love and encouragement brought me through it, and the Holy Spirit was like a warm cleansing oil within my heart.

Time passed and I was transferred to Saughton Prison in Edinburgh. There the Lord moved the healing process forward again by prompting me to confide in someone else. This time it was to a lady called Elizabeth, whom I'd met at the Prison Fellowship weekend when I was converted.

The Lord helped me to tell her all that was in my heart, and her patience and gentleness brought down many barriers that still needed working on. I now count her as a very dear friend, one who will always remain special. Her visits are still important to me.

But God knew that the healing process was still not complete, and he brought another lady from Prison

Fellowship into my life. Her name was Mollie. Through our times of sharing and praying together, the Lord has continued to 'put me together' again.

The Prison Fellowship meetings in Saughton also encourage me in my faith. Brought up as a Catholic, I attend Mass - but I also sing in the Church of Scotland choir! I don't think Jesus is small enough to fit into a denominational box. At Prison Fellowship there is a spirit of love which draws together everybody who loves Jesus, whether they be Catholic or Protestant. In this atmosphere of love, doctrinal issues become secondary.

I have been a Christian just over six years now. I have written about what Christ has done in my life, but I don't think I am now 'whiter than snow'. I can echo what David wrote in Psalm 51: 'My sin is ever before me'. But equally, I can say I have been given 'a new heart'. And as I give my heart to God each day, I know he will continue to change me, for there is still a great deal of work to be done in my life. But 'God is faithful and he will do it.'

This is a story, not of my sin nor of my brokenness, but of God's healing love. This love reaches a depth I never knew outside prison. This love has set me free behind prison bars. May God bless all who read this book, and may his guiding hand remain on the Prison Fellowship ministry which offers 'freedom for the prisoners'.

* * * * *

As Peter indicated, Chaplains are part of the team who try to help. In the next chapter James Jack, otherwise known as 'The Rev', gives us his impressions ...

> 'Do not be anxious about anything, but in everything, by prayer and petition, with thanksgiving, present your requests to God. And the peace of God, which transcends all understanding, will guard your hearts and your minds in Christ Jesus' (Philippians 4:6,7).

9

TO PEACE THROUGH PRAYER
by James 'The Rev' Jack,
Chaplain
H.M. Young Offenders' Institution,
Castle Huntly

Inspired by John Bunyan's book, Pilgrim's Progress, the text and title of this chapter are to be seen as signposts for a journey which begins at a time and place of 'Worry' and ends at a place of 'Peace'. The way to 'Peace' is sometimes long and difficult. Some travellers try to ignore the signposts and try to find their own way there, using the way of 'Human Understanding'. But all roads off the 'King's Way' usually lead to the place of 'Disaster'. For the way to 'Peace' lies far beyond 'Human Understanding' and is only reachable through 'Prayer'. This chapter is an exploration of such a journey where some travellers are looking for 'Peace' and encounter those on the path of 'Prayer'.

'If only it were possible to spend a whole day with the inmates, then perhaps we could be more effective!'

Dr. Sheila Lenman's remark echoed the feelings of each member of the group. It was Wednesday and they were meeting as usual to pray for the prisoners and staff of Castle Huntly Young Offenders' Institution near Dundee. This evening was slightly different because, as Chaplain-to-be of that institution, I had been invited to join them.

I knew that another group of Prison Fellowship volunteers met in Dundee every month for the same purpose and I was encouraged at the outset by the thought of the support of these committed Christians who had been praying for the prison for many years.

That evening I learned that the previous Chaplain had first invited Dr. Lenman to come into the prison to conduct a mid-week Bible study group. As I looked round the group it was obvious that their commitment, ideas and enthusiasm would prevent my task of becoming a Prison Chaplain for the first time from being a solitary one.

I have been at Castle Huntly for four years now, and I've discovered a few common characteristics of the men who are inmates here.

Aged between sixteen and twenty-one, most have been convicted for theft, committed in order to finance an alcohol or drug habit. Many have been drinking since they were ten or eleven years old. They drink to escape from the reality of their lives which all too often involve family problems - parents separating; physical or sexual abuse; bullying. And so, unwanted, unloved, and unable to cope, they arrive at Castle Huntly.

As a Chaplain I long to tell them that Jesus can enter into the blackest of situations and change things. The tragedy is that many inmates resign themselves to lives of crime because no-one has ever shown them anything else. So how can we help them? Let me tell you about some of the attempts we are making ...

Some time ago, Sheila Lenman contacted some Christian students at St. Andrews University, and asked if they would like to come and share in the leading of our Sunday meeting. We now have a group of about twenty students who come every fortnight during term time on Sunday evenings. These young men and women come from various faculties of the University, and the mix of students and inmates has worked extremely well over the past few years - due no doubt to the fact that the students regularly pray together, especially before going into the prison. Some of the students hope to go into full-time Christian ministries. Perhaps they too are challenged by our Sunday evening get-togethers.

Sometimes we break into small groups and discuss a theme - whatever the inmates want to discuss. Topics have ranged from 'The divinity of Christ' to 'Sex before marriage'. Debate is always lively and the inmates love it.

But we are not limited to debates. Some of the inmates have been willing to sing, share their faith, play musical instruments and pray for people in hospital.

On one occasion the inmates made a collection to buy a toy and a 'Get Well' card for a three-year-old girl who was in hospital diagnosed as having leukaemia. This touched me personally, as the little girl was my niece, Hazel. They had somehow found out the dilemma our family was facing and, on their own initiative, they did something practical to help. For many weeks afterwards, inmates quietly approached me to ask about Hazel. Several of them said they were remembering her in prayer. They are learning that prayer is practical and effective.

With Prison Fellowship's support we have encouraged other young people to become visitors in Castle Huntly. Some from my own congregation and some from neighbouring 'Teen Ranch' join with the St. Andrews students on Sundays and Wednesdays. Still other schemes involve Christians from other age groups.

In order to increase involvement between the Young Offenders and the community, we have started a Visitor Centre, staffed by thirty ladies from local congregations, assisted by the Womens Royal Voluntary Service. Through this scheme the prison teacher can call upon local Christians to help with basic reading skills, and local congregations can donate Christmas gifts for the children of inmates.

One idea, which grew from a comment made at my first meeting with the Prison Fellowship group, has now become an annual feature, and takes place at Easter. With the Governor's permission - and a team of around fifty visitors - we stage an all day event. The morning session opens with worship followed by a football tournament, culminating with the best visiting team playing the best prison team.

After lunch we break up into MAD workshops [Music, Art and Drama], and come back together at the end of the afternoon. We have had a variety of guest speakers including a reformed alcoholic Christian from Glasgow, a former US Naval Marine and a Scottish Premier Division football player.

In the evening we usually have a live band. Once I booked a band from Govanhill in Glasgow. When they started to play the noise was so loud that I slipped out, leaving the fifty visitors and ninety inmates to enjoy the 'music'. I wandered over to the prison recreation room where I found an officer playing table tennis with an inmate. Two other inmates were standing watching. I joined them, saying nothing.

A few minutes later the man beside me, 'Big Wullie', asked if he could talk to me. Rather surprised, I took him to a small interview room where he proceeded to pour out a catalogue of fears. It seemed the local gang were out to get him when he was released. Obviously we would need to try to find an alternative place for him to stay.

But he still hadn't finished his story.

'I have an evil spirit in me,' he said. 'That's why I was so violent last night. It's not like me at all.'

This boy had never been to any of our Easter seminars and had never shown any interest in the worship or mid-week Bible Class.

'If you think you have a spiritual problem, then you'd better look for a spiritual answer, hadn't you?' I answered. 'God could help you. Would you like me to pray with you?'

'Yes please.' I stood beside him, laid my hands upon his head and prayed with him. He turned to me, smiling for the first time.

'How did you pray like that?' he asked.

'You can pray like that too,' I assured him. Then, as we continued to speak together, we both noticed that his voice had changed somehow. All the signs of frustration, fear and hatefulness had been removed. The simple prayer had brought him peace. I urged him to try to live out that peace in prison.

It was the first time that anything like this had ever happened in my ministry. I hurried back to the Hall to tell someone about it. But before I could start my story, Liz, a member of Prison Fellowship met me.

'I've been reading a Psalm,' she said, 'and I'm sure verse eleven would help one of the inmates. But I don't know which one.'

We found a Bible and looked up Psalm 36 and together read verse eleven. 'May the foot of the proud not come against me, nor the hand of the wicked drive me away'.

I certainly knew who that verse was for! Just two weeks later Big Wullie came to a Bible Study group and told the other members of his newly found faith.

Another area in which I find Prison Fellowship to be so helpful is in the aftercare of inmates. They have a national network of people who are experienced in dealing with offenders, and I am often glad to be able to tap into this resource. If possible I try to arrange a meeting between a Prison Fellowship contact and an inmate about to be discharged so that, later on, they can meet outside and hopefully the ex-offender can be taken into a caring church fellowship.

We have learned to pray regularly for all inmates. Many have been converted. Some fall away as soon as they are released. Some who have fallen away, come back into fellowship later on. Some become Christians years after leaving Castle Huntly. Some persevere and start to grapple with the real issues in their lives and allow God to make them a 'new creation'.

One lad, Jimmy, came into Castle Huntly convicted of a drugs charge. He was so wrapped up in himself that no one else mattered. His wife and two children took second place. Of the many hundreds of inmates I have met, he is the only one who made me angry. He told me frankly that he was in control of his life and had no need of God. Whatever I said simply slid off his slimy attitude to life. He was not a very nice person - and I hoped I would never meet him again.

Several months later I walked into the institution and found Jimmy waiting to see me.

'I'm here to meet the new inmates,' I said shortly. 'You'll have to wait.'

'But I am a new inmate,' he replied, surprising me. It seemed he had been caught re-offending shortly after his release. But something about Jimmy was different - he seemed broken somehow. All his arrogance had disappeared - he even asked if he could come to the Bible class! He had realised that his way hadn't worked and now he was looking for another way.

About this time Dr. Billy Graham came to Scotland. I was planning to take some of my parishioners to the rally at Murrayfield, Edinburgh. As we still had some empty seats on the bus, I asked the Governor of Castle Huntly if we could take some inmates to the rally with us. I thought perhaps he might allow one or two to come, but I didn't dare hope for more.

'How many empty seats have you?' he enquired.

'Sixteen,' I replied.

'Right,' he said. 'Fill them up with the inmates.'

Jimmy was one of the sixteen allowed to come with us.

Again Prison Fellowship stepped in to help as escorts. I had imagined us all needing to keep together in a secure bunch, but on the day, our bus had to park two miles from the stadium. As we were walking along the streets of Edinburgh, we got split up in the crowds heading to hear Dr. Graham. Some of the inmates spotted a petrol station open and needed to use the toilet facilities. Others queued for ice cream, and before we got to the stadium all but four of the boys were missing! I was quite convinced that my head was on the chopping block.

In the stadium I could not listen to a word Dr. Graham said, but quietly prayed for a miracle to happen. And it did!

I had volunteered to act as one of the Mission Scotland Counsellors, so when Dr. Graham called for enquirers to go onto the playing field, I went along with them. I remember looking around the stadium to see if I could see any of the inmates in the crowd, but there were too many people.

I needn't have worried. Standing right beside me were eight of the boys who had responded to Dr. Graham's call and come forward for counselling! Later I escorted them back to the bus, still wondering about the others. To my great relief they were all waiting for us in the bus. On the way home Jimmy told me he had committed his life to Christ.

'My marriage is over, so I can't go back home,' he said. 'I shall just have to make a new start.'

Fortunately when Jimmy was released we were able to direct him to accommodation with a Christian family in a different area. They have adopted him as their own and encouraged him in his new faith.

The work of Prison Fellowship is an integral part of our overall mission at Castle Huntly and we have developed a team ministry of over seventy people. Our prisons are richer places because of their presence and I cannot imagine not having them around to provide spiritual support for prisoners, staff, chaplains and our families.

* * * * *

Hamish Ross is a Prison Governor. God moved him from Scotland to the Persian Gulf and then back to Scotland. His story shows how God was controlling each move so as to have his man in the right place at the right time for the work he wanted him to do...

> 'And what does the LORD require of you? To act justly and to love mercy and to walk humbly with your God' (Micah 6:8).

10

A GOVERNOR ON THE TEAM
by Hamish Ross
Prison Governor,
H.M. Prison, Penninghame

In January, 1970, I left the RAF in which I had served for half my life. Those years held happy memories for me, for I had made many friends. Indeed, it was during my RAF service that I met my best friend - the Lord Jesus Christ.

It happened through SASRA - Soldiers and Airmen's Scripture Readers' Association. This fine Christian organisation not only encourages Christian servicemen and women in their spiritual lives, but it can link them with other Christians serving in the Armed Forces, on a worldwide basis.

When I was posted from RAF Kinloss, Moray, to RAF Sharjah in the United Arab Emirates in the Persian Gulf, SASRA gave me the name and address of the SASRA Branch Secretary in Sharjah and also sent him my particulars.

When my friend, Donald, and I arrived in Sharjah, we were bused around the RAF section with about twenty other airmen, in search of accommodation. The driver had a list of vacancies and, as we passed various groups of billets, he shouted out the appropriate number of vacant beds and allowed time for a matching number of sweating airmen to alight.

'W20' was a four-man room, and when our knowledgeable driver informed us that two of the beds were vacant, Donald and I jumped off the bus and entered what was to be our home for most of the next year.

A few minutes later as we were settling in, Donald nodded to one of the other beds.

'Looks like there's one of yours in here,' he said, pointing to a Bible on one of the lockers. When I went across to check his locker card I discovered it was none other than my SASRA contact!

His name was Paul, and the fellowship we enjoyed together made all the difference to my time in Sharjah. It also gave me first-hand experience of an organisation which allowed 'all ranks' to share fellowship together in Christ, unwittingly preparing me for Prison Fellowship in the future.

After leaving the RAF I joined the Scottish Prison Service. I collected my accoutrements - whistle, key chain and baton - and tried to settle into the sometimes peculiar ways of my new environment.

I soon discovered that the gospel story was being told in every prison and institution. Chaplains conducted services each Sunday, and if their limited hours in the prison permitted, they tried to interview every new inmate. They also saw prisoners who had asked to speak to them, and a number of them spent time walking round the workshops and halls, talking to staff and prisoners. I have always seen this as a particularly important part of a Chaplain's role, for their neutrality eases the way for friendly contact.

I also found that there were a number of Bible Classes in operation, mostly on Sunday afternoons. They were run by a variety of Christian people who came from different churches, and they had two good points - they wanted to talk about Jesus, and they gave their services free of charge!

In addition, I noticed that some individual members of staff tried to introduce their colleagues and charges to Christ by the way they lived. And I remembered the advice an ex-Governor had given me when I was about to join the Prison Service.

'Join to do a good job, not evangelise,' he said. He knew that, to do a job well was in itself a form of evangelising. And he also knew how closely prisoners watch staff, and how they respond to a job well done!

By all these various means men and women were hearing, many for the first time, about a Saviour who was interested in and loved them, and some committed their lives to him. It is never an easy decision to live for Christ in prison and, from my time in the forces, I knew something of what they had to endure.

I soon became aware of the problems which arose when Christian prisoners were released or transferred to other prisons. Chaplains were able to get in touch with fellow ministers and tell them who was to be released; Bible class leaders could sometimes provide contacts within their own churches. But all too often, valued and interested ex-offenders just 'vanished' as far as the Christian church was concerned. This was mainly due to poor communication between people working inside the prisons, and the churches on the 'outside'. There was also a great shortage of caring people willing to help inmates' families and the prisoners themselves when they were released.

It was against this background of ongoing, but often haphazard work, that in June 1981, while serving at Polmont Borstal, I received an invitation. John Marsburgh, a prison officer, friend and fellow Christian, told me about a meeting of concerned Christians who were interested in Prison Ministry in Scotland. He asked if I would like to attend. I agreed, and we both presented ourselves at Gilmerton House in Fife to see what it was all about.

We were warmly welcomed by our delightful hostess, the most Scottish of all Americans, Louise Purvis, and I was immediately impressed by the eagerness of those gathered in the lovely drawing room. I have to admit that I was concerned at that time about the prospect of so many 'keen amateurs' being involved in prison work, to say nothing of the American and English connections of Prison Fellowship! I was reassured, however, by the presence of two Prison Social Workers, Helena Bryce and Angus Creighton, and another prison officer, Derek Watt. I felt they added a touch of reality to the situation!

You will already have read details of that meeting in an earlier chapter. It was good to discuss the concept of Christian life in the prison system in a practical way, with the ideas of Prison Fellowship in mind. I happily became part of the resultant core group. During the following months Prison Fellowship was born and grew steadily - always aiming to be in favour with God, but finding out just how difficult it could be to be in favour with man!

From my point of view, by far the most delicate task which fell to me was to present Prison Fellowship Scotland as a credible organisation to Prison Governors - though after meeting Chuck Colson, most of them were willing to involve Prison Fellowship in their establishments. Their tolerance with some early 'hiccups' was greatly appreciated. They were no doubt reassured by the knowledge that Prison Fellowship carefully selected and trained its volunteers in the various prisons.

I also had to introduce this 'new baby' to the Chaplains and groups of faithful Christians who had been running Bible Classes in the prisons for years. Some had been working there for decades before Prison Fellowship was founded - one leader had conducted a Bible study for well over twenty years!

But from a Governor's perspective, I could see that Prison Fellowship Scotland would introduce a number of desirable spiritual features into the Scottish Prison Service. First, it would provide a network capable of matching released prisoners with a church or fellowship which could offer support to them and their families. Secondly, it would provide a Christian link for prisoners who were transferred from one prison to another. The Chaplain and Prison Fellowship Group working in one prison could be informed in advance about an inmate being transferred, and he could be welcomed into his new prison. Prison Fellowship would become an extended family to many inmates, as it provided continuity of care both inside prison and out.

As time went by, a number of my Governor colleagues began to contact me with queries about Prison Fellowship and its work. In most cases I was able to advise and inform them - or even reassure them if need be. Their queries and attitudes were as varied and colourful as the Governors themselves. Some had a personal Christian commitment and therefore a greater interest in the spiritual side of Prison Fellowship. Others denied any spiritual interest - though I didn't believe all of them! They had a purely professional interest, wanting to utilise Prison Fellowship Scotland as another resource for their Chaplains and prisons. They saw it as a way of developing the Fellowship groups: finding volunteers who would write letters; visit prisoners; provide concerts and Fellowship weekends; send in Christian books, cassettes and videos; follow up ex-prisoners; work with prisoners' families; and provide prayer support for prisoners and staff.

At present the Scottish Prison Service is passing through a time of great change, trying to develop a number of key initiatives and concepts. Prison Fellowship Scotland still aims, with God's guidance, to fit in with these changes; to organise for the excellence and glory of God, and to present the good news that Jesus Christ is a responsive and life-changing Saviour. It is a privilege to be on their team.

* * * * *

This life-changing Saviour picked Cokey Cochrane up from the gutter ... or so he says.

11

FROM THE GUTTER TO GRACE
by Michael 'Cokey' Cochrane,
Ex-inmate

My life of crime began at a very early age with all kinds
of minor offences - I broke into schools, stole from shops
and did just about every petty crime you can think of. I
was smoking from the age of eight, skipping school,
running away from home, and generally being disobedi-
ent. By the time I was fourteen I found myself in a List
'D' school for assaulting and robbing a milk boy.

As I got older my crimes became more serious. I had
developed a tremendous craving for alcohol and was
drinking heavily. For a couple of years there was hardly
a weekend when I didn't end up fighting and land myself
in jail.

I got married when I was eighteen because my girlfriend was pregnant. Family pressure and public opinion
hurried me into the marriage, persuading me that it was
the right thing to do. During the ceremony I made vows
before a God I didn't know.

I did believe there was a God - I'd been brought up a
Catholic and gone through all the traditional ceremonies
- infant baptism, Holy Communion and confirmation. I'd
also heard stories about Jesus in primary school. But

none of that meant that I 'knew' God.

He always seemed so far away, except for times when I had a desperate problem, or ended up in jail. Then I'd pray and ask him to help me out. I'd tell him how sorry I was and promise never to do whatever it was again. But somehow I never seemed able to keep the promises I made to God. It was as if my whole lifestyle and nature prevented me. The Bible is right when it says that our very nature is sinful and cannot please God.

My marriage produced two children but by the age of twenty-two I was divorced. By this time drugs had become the most important thing in my life. I still drank heavily, but drugs had taken the dominant role. I was selling cannabis, speed, LSD and cocaine to earn my living. At the same time I was involved in setting up and carrying out serious crimes such as robberies and wage snatches. The whole driving force in my life was to make money to keep my drug habit supplied. But deep inside I was really empty. I was living in a false world but I couldn't break free from it. I was trapped.

For the next two years I had a relationship with a girl and was in and of prison several times. At that time the most important things to me were my lifestyle, my girlfriend and my house.

Then in 1985 I found myself lying in a police station in Oban, charged with 'assault to the danger of life'. Three of us were charged and we all got bail, but something inside me told me that I would be going to jail again for this offence. It meant I would have to go to the High Court.

That in itself sobered me up, but by the time I got my date to go to court, I was already in Low Moss prison doing six months. I discovered that my two friends were turning 'Queen's evidence' against me.

My relationship was on its last legs and I knew it would break up if I got the jail again. My only hope of getting off was to lie through my back teeth. This shouldn't have been any bother, as I'd lied in and out of courtrooms for years!

This time, however, things were different. I couldn't explain what was happening to me, but I had been reading a book called *Snatched From The Flames* by Anita Hyde, who worked with a group called Prison Fellowship in England. It was the story of a young girl whose life seemed to have taken the same course as mine - crime, drugs, prisons. All I know was that every night as I read the pages of that book, I was in tears - me, a twenty-five year old 'tough guy', sobbing like a big baby!

At the time I didn't understand what was happening to me, but God was showing me all my faults, my sins, my selfishness, my lack of consideration for other people and their property. He showed me that even in my relationship, I was selfish.

I was completely broken up inside. I found I couldn't pray and ask God to get me out this time. I was becoming more conscious of him and the more conscious I became, the more dirt I saw in myself. I knew I deserved to go to jail, so I went to the trial and told the truth. I had been praying that I wouldn't get sentenced to more than three years, though of course I didn't want to go to jail at all. But God's Holy Spirit convicted me, and I prayed to him for mercy. I knew I could easily be sentenced to five years or more, but in fact I got thirty months. As I was already doing six months, that added up to three years!

God's judgment was just and right and justice was done. We need to be careful how we pray sometimes - I asked God for justice, and justice was done. (I used to think justice was when you got away with something!)

I was taken to Barlinnie and put in 'A' hall. A couple of days later one of my mates introduced me to a guy he knew. After walking in the exercise yard one day we went upstairs to his cell. We were having a bit of idle chatter about who he knew from Paisley - where I come from - and who I knew from Pollock - where he came from - when I noticed he had a Bible by his bed. It's not every day you see someone in jail with a Bible in their cell. It's just not the 'in' thing. Most people had crime books, porn magazines, murder stories - that seemed to be what most guys wanted.

At that point only God and myself had any idea what was happening in my life, but I eventually managed to pluck up courage to ask if I could borrow his Bible. To my surprise he began to tell me that he was a 'born again' Christian and that he had come to know Jesus as his Saviour during his sentence.

It is amazing how God puts just the right person across your path at just the right time. This guy gave me a Bible and encouraged me to read it. He also gave me some leaflets about the persecuted Church in Russia, which showed me that people were being imprisoned and tortured because of their confession of faith in the Lord Jesus Christ. These people were being treated worse than me, and they had committed no crime.

I knew nothing about the Bible. I didn't know where to begin. I never knew the Old Testament was at the front and the New Testament was at the back! I never knew that the four Gospels of Matthew, Mark, Luke and John were records of Jesus' life while he was on earth, or that all the letters in the rest of the New Testament were written for our instruction. I never knew that the Bible was God's written word of revelation to mankind. The leaflet told me to look at John 15, so I turned to page fifteen only to find it was in Genesis. I had a lot to learn!

I thank God that there were people in the prison who did know about these things and could help me. I discovered that a group of Prison Fellowship volunteers came into the prison every week and they encouraged prisoners to read the Bible and put their trust in Jesus.

I acquired a small book, the Gospel of Luke. I must have read it three or four times. It was so exciting and so real. I started going to the Prison Fellowship meetings and, through that and my reading of the Gospel, I became aware for the first time that I needed to commit my life to Jesus and to trust him personally as my Saviour and Lord.

But I was scared to ask Jesus into my heart and life because it would mean a big change!

Even though I knew I deserved the jail and was beginning to see God's hand in the whole thing, I still didn't want to forgive the two pals who had turned evidence against me. But I knew I would have to forgive them, because Jesus had forgiven me all my sins.

A battle raged inside me. I knew I was a sinner and I knew I couldn't change myself. I knew the jail couldn't change me or make me any better, but I did know that Jesus could do in me what I couldn't do myself.

I read in the Bible in Romans 10:13 that 'Everyone who calls upon the name of the Lord will be saved'; in John 1:12 it said, 'to all who received him, to those who believed in his name, he gave the right to become children of God.' Also in John 3:16, it said, 'For God so loved the world that he gave his one and only Son, that whoever believes in him shall not perish but have eternal life.' So I called upon the Lord and received Jesus into my heart as my Lord and Saviour.

I had this weird, preconceived idea that when I did this, all my problems were just going to disappear! But Jesus did not die to take my problems away. He died to take my sins away and to set me free from the power of sin. The Lord began to work out of me all the rubbish that the world had pumped into me over the years. Everything was not rosy all the time. There were hard times - troubles, sorrows, pains and trials, as the Lord took away from me all the things I had depended on, so that I would learn to depend on him.

Within a few weeks there was a riot at Barlinnie and I was moved to Greenock prison. At that time I was still smoking and occasionally took a bit of dope, though I knew God was wanting to release me from it. So one Friday night I prayed and asked God to take away the desire for dope.

That weekend I was allowed out for a visit and I brought five pounds worth of coins back into the jail. I was caught, put on report, lost seven days remission and had my open visits taken away from me for three months. Even though I didn't like losing my open visits, I believe God used it to break my desire for dope. Without the money, I couldn't get any. He was answering my prayers his way!

My relationship came to an end soon after that and it seemed as if everything that could go wrong in my life was doing so. Then I remembered that my life really didn't belong to me any more - it belonged to Christ. I had been 'bought with a price.' I found that God's grace sustained me through all the hard times.

I started to attend the Prison Fellowship meetings as often as I could. Many a time I would want to ask a question, but I just didn't have the courage. But God never let me down. Before the meeting was over, someone else would ask the same question and I'd get my answer.

I received great encouragement from the Fellowship team at Greenock. I didn't know what lay ahead of me, but God did. When Greenock closed down and became a Young Offenders' Institution some months later, I realised just how much I had benefited from being there. God had done a lot of work in my life in those six months.

I was next sent to Shotts Prison. Shotts had been opened just two weeks previously and the whole system was in an upheaval. Prisoners came flooding in from prisons all over the country and all the guys who had been attending Prison Fellowship in other prisons suddenly found themselves all together. It was great!

By this time I had discovered that the devil didn't have two horns and a long pointed tail, as some people imagine. But he was real enough - an enemy from hell itself, who still wanted to destroy my soul and my life. But I didn't belong to him any more. I was beginning to see that the battles which were going on in my life were spiritual battles. I read in Ephesians 6:12 that 'our struggle is not against flesh and blood, but against the rulers ... against the powers of this dark world and against the spiritual forces of evil in the heavenly realms.' God was revealing these truths to me and I had to take my stand as a Christian.

These truths were all basic instruction from the Bible - yet I had never heard them before. I wondered why others - especially those one would have expected to know - never seemed to know these truths either? When I tried to tell some of these people about the things God was doing in my life and all the things he was showing me, it was as if they just couldn't understand. Yet to me it seemed so simple. But their attitude proved Saint Paul was right when he wrote in 2 Corinthians 4:4 that 'the God of this age has blinded the minds of unbelievers, so that they cannot see the light of the gospel of the glory of Christ.'

In Shotts, Prison Fellowship met on Thursday nights and it was always encouraging. We spent some time just worshipping the Lord, some time in prayer and then we received instruction from the Word of God. As 2 Timothy 3:16 says: God's word 'is useful for teaching, rebuking, correcting and training in righteousness,' and I found this to be true. We also took time to encourage one another by telling what had happened to us that week.

It was around that time that I became aware that God wanted to give me a gift of the Holy Spirit. In the book of Acts, it says that 'you will receive power when the Holy Spirit comes upon you and you will be his witnesses'. So how do I get this Holy Spirit? I wondered. Then I discovered that Jesus himself said that his Father would give the Holy Spirit to those ask him (Luke 11:13). So I asked, and received the Holy Spirit, just as God promised.

While I was in Shotts I re-established contact with a

Christian friend whom I had known for years. He visited me every week and was a great encouragement spiritually. He was closely involved with a Christian Fellowship in Paisley and hoped to link me up with some of its members. This was mid-October, 1987.

A month later I heard that I was to be moved to Noranside Prison for the last six months of my sentence. I had actually applied to go there earlier, but had been refused. I had accepted it as God's will for me at that time.

But when I moved to Noranside at the end of January 1988, I learned that two inmates and a couple of ladies in the Prison Fellowship group at Noranside had been praying for Christians to be sent there! So although the prison authorities wouldn't let me go there when I first applied, no authority could stop me from going when God's people prayed!

Prison Fellowship in Noranside met once a week. There were small groups of people who came into the prison to encourage us and we were very grateful for their faithfulness. Colin Cuthbert, Prison Fellowship Director, also visited us from time to time to let us know what was happening in the other in-prison Fellowship groups which some of us had attended in the past.

It seems sad that so many people fail to receive the blessing that God has for them. Some inmates would not go to Prison Fellowship meetings for fear that their friends would laugh or call them names. Some people accused me of being a Christian so that I could get parole. What a load of rubbish! I never got parole. Neither did I get anything else out of the prison system, but I did receive grace and freedom from God through Christ Jesus.

When I was released for two weekends from Saturday to Sunday night, my Christian friend took me to a meeting in Paisley. This gave me the opportunity to meet other Christians from my home town. I feel it is most important for Christian prisoners to try to establish some link with a local fellowship before they are released if at all possible.

When the time came for my release, I looked back at the past few years of my life - from Low Moss to Barlinnie ... Greenock ... Shotts and Noranside. The Lord sure passed me around a bit, but I believe it was for his purpose and glory.

I have been out of jail for five years now and there have been ups and downs, but the Lord has kept me. In July 1990 I married a young lady I met in the church I attend in Paisley.

Not long before we were married the Lord gave me the opportunity of a trip to Africa. I went to Zimbabwe and Tanzania for eight weeks in all. There I saw people who were spiritually hungry for the Word of God. Here I see the Word of God widely available, but people just don't seem to want it.

I now have the opportunity and privilege of going back into prisons occasionally as a Prison Fellowship volunteer to talk to some of the men inside and to assure them that there is hope.

I remember only too often thinking: 'It's all right for those people that come in with Prison Fellowship, visiting and then being able to go away again back outside. They don't know what it's like having to go back to a cell.'

If you are an inmate, maybe you think like that

sometimes. But stop and think again. These people are ordinary men and women who are sacrificing their time in order to encourage you. They're giving you the opportunity to know their Lord and Saviour, Jesus.

I know I personally am indebted to many people in Prison Fellowship Scotland - those in the ministry team; those who visited me; those who are part of prayer support groups. I would encourage them to remember that their 'labour in the Lord is not in vain'. My changed life is proof of that.

From the gutter to God's grace may seem a long distance, but in reality it is only one heartfelt prayer away.

*****

Cokey's story shows that prayer is a vital feature in all Prison Fellowship groups. The next chapter confirms this. Marion Watt visits Gateside Prison in Greenock where her husband, Derek, is a Prison Officer. If we let him start the ball rolling, then she can have the last word!

12

FROM THE HAND OF THE FOE
by Derek Watt, Prison Officer
and Marion Watt
Prison Fellowship,
H.M. Prison Gateside, Greenock

Part one - Derek's story

As a young man in my early twenties I was walking home from a Bible study with a friend, Ian, who had recently become a Christian, when out of the blue he asked: 'Derek, have you ever thought about the Prison Service? I think Christians like you should be involved in these kind of jobs.'

'It's never crossed my mind,' I said. 'I don't know a thing about it. I don't even know anybody who's been near a prison.'

Besides, I thought, I don't think I'd be suitable for work like that. I was settled in the job I had with a national meat distribution company. The work was hard, starting early in the mornings and lasting fairly long hours, but I'd never thought of looking for anything else. So I dismissed what Ian had said. Or I thought I did. Trouble was, the seed had been sown! And the idea stayed with me - so much so that I decided to send for an application form for the Prison Service.

At the same time I prayed about it. I suppose my prayer went something like this: 'Lord, if it is not your will for me to work in the Prison Service, prevent the application from being accepted, or let me fail the exam, the medical, or the interview.' I wanted to do God's will, whatever, so I left the outcome with him.

One of the questions on the application form was: 'State your reason for wishing to join the Prison Service.' My answer: 'To share my Christian faith with those in prison.'

My application was accepted! I was then ordered to report to Peterhead Prison to sit an exam, have a medical and be interviewed by a Governor and a Chief Officer. Even after twenty-five years I can still remember my feelings and reactions as I walked through the small wicket gate into the muster area. I was scared stiff!

Staff were arriving to take up duty and to me they looked like giants. Compared to them I felt puny and absolutely unsuitable. No-one spoke to me.

The small wicket gate opened again and an officer with a braided hat walked through it. He had a scar running down one side of his face and he looked as if he had been hewn out of granite.

'I bet nobody messes about with him,' I thought.

Then someone said 'Hello Boris,' and he nodded his head. The large gate was opened, and the staff marched through to take up their posts.

That was my first meeting with Chief Officer Campbell, a man respected throughout the service by staff and prisoners alike.

I met him again at my interview two hours later when he and the Governor had to determine whether I was a realistic, practical individual or just a do-gooder. It was possibly the first time in my life that I had to give a reasonable account of my faith.

Neither man was anti-Christian, but both had come up against Christians who had done more harm than good inside prison. The 'Jim Taylor troubles' were playing havoc in the north of Scotland at the time, especially in the Peterhead area, and Christians were definitely not the flavour of the month!

That same day I had my first encounter with a prisoner. I was told to go up a flight of stairs for my medical. A prisoner was on his knees polishing the stairs, so I excused myself, apologised for walking over his work, and asked him how he was. I am still waiting for an answer!

But the look he gave me told me everything - it was full of hatred. It was a rude awakening for me, and it hurt. After all, I was joining the Service to help these lads, and I thought they should have known this! My 'call' was almost 'called off' there and then!

I had been in the Prison Service for fifteen years when Prison Fellowship began to function. At the time I was running a Bible Class at Cornton Vale, Scotland's only women's prison. A team of local Christians came in to help, and quite a number of women inmates attended.

Then I was invited by Louise Purvis to join other interested Christians at her home to consider setting up Prison Fellowship in Scotland. What really impressed me about that meeting was the vision of the 'core group'. It was an answer to prayer. I knew that Christian work in prisons was growing, but I was increasingly concerned about what happened to new converts when they were released from prison. They were going out of Cornton Vale to their homes throughout Scotland, but we had no way of following them up.

Now this group of people were about to set up an organisation to deal with this very problem! I believed then, as I do now, that Prison Fellowship was not just a good idea but the leading of the Spirit of God. My involvement with Prison Fellowship began that day and has continued to the present.

Chuck Colson's vision of 'prisoner evangelising prisoner' really took hold of me. It changed both my understanding and my way of doing things. The gospel had been preached in prisons for many years and would continue to be - but having a Fellowship inside prison, though not new in principle, would certainly be new in practice.

In 1986 I was transferred to a new prison - Gateside, in Greenock. It was an anxious time in the Scottish Prison Service. There had been a number of riots throughout Scotland, and when it opened, Greenock was to receive some of the long-term prisoners from all over the country who had been involved in the riots.

The Governor there was a Christian and asked me if I would start a Prison Fellowship group. For the first time in my experience I found I would be working alongside a fellow officer who was a Christian. Ian Lynch had been transferred from Barlinnie, and his enthusiasm for Prison Fellowship was inspirational. So we gathered together a team of Christians to come into the prison and help. Some of them are with us to this day. Every Wednesday evening and every Sunday afternoon, Billy Paul, Louis Reynolds and a large team come in and have fellowship with the prisoners. Only God can - and will - assess the value of their faithfulness.

The first Prison Fellowship meetings with our new inmate population were different to anything I have ever experienced. Some prisoners had become Christians while in other prisons, but the majority were not Christians. The meetings were rather 'hairy' to say the least. There was anger, bitterness and hatred - some between inmate and inmate, some directed towards staff. There were times when we expected the place to explode. But out of it all grew real fellowship. Men who had been bitter enemies publicly apologised to each other. Some of the hardest and most troublesome prisoners, who still have considerable time to do before their release, stood up in front of their colleagues and prayed. Their language, even in prayer, was 'choice', but the Lord knew their hearts and heard their prayers.

At the end of our Fellowship time we held hands and repeated the Lord's Prayer together. What a motley crew we were - sex offenders, murderers, bank robbers, drug pushers and dealers, Prison Officers and the Prison Fellowship team. Who would believe such a gathering could happen?

Trouble continued in Scottish prisons, but not in Greenock. One Governor commented: 'I believe the reason there is relative quiet at Greenock is in part due to the Christian community within the prison.' This was the Christian community acting as 'salt and light' in the world, as Jesus said they should.

Two years later Greenock changed from being a long-term adult prison to a long-term Young Offenders' Institution. It was a bit like starting all over again. We had become used to fairly high numbers of adults attending the Fellowship, but we dropped down to six or seven.

At one point there was a short overlap when not all the adult prisoners had left. A couple of the older men who were regular Fellowship attenders asked if they could address the Young Offenders in the dining hall to tell them about Prison Fellowship and encourage them to attend. This was really 'prisoner evangelising prisoner' and it was successful. After that our numbers grew quite dramatically.

We were soon faced with another problem which has been one of the most difficult to resolve: the problem of sex offenders. The policy under our Governor was that all the Young Offenders, whatever their offence, should be able to do their sentence as normally as possible. That meant all prisoners were together 'in association', attending Education, PE classes and, of course, Prison Fellowship.

Our meetings took a fairly traditional form. We sat in a circle hoping this would encourage fellowship among those who wanted it. But it posed problems for those who found it impossible to sit next to someone who had committed a sex offence.

We resolved the issue by operating the Fellowship as a coffee bar. We set tables with milk, sugar and biscuits and let the lads choose whom they wished to sit beside. The Team then served the coffee and joined the lads at the tables where they could all chat informally.

It was normal for about fifty or sixty young men to meet with us twice a week. In fact the Governor felt it wise to put a ceiling on the numbers attending in case things got out of control. The only staff present would be

Ian and myself, backed up by a team of around twelve Prison Fellowship volunteers. This set-up lasted for two years, and for me they were the most profitable years I have enjoyed in the Service. Many lads became Christians and we are still in touch with some of them. As a team we learned a great deal about communicating our faith.

Greenock is now a local prison, holding men doing fairly short sentences, and also men and young lads waiting to go to court. We have a Fellowship on Wednesday for the convicted prisoners and on Sunday afternoon for the untried inmates. We continue the coffee bar style. We find this is a way that allows greater opportunity for small group work and one to one contact, and it does not in any way spoil the effect on the occasions when we have someone in to speak.

Years ago I heard Chuck Colson say that the Chinese word for prison was 'Hell-Hole'. Not knowing Chinese, I can't say if he was right or not, but it is a fairly accurate description of prisons worldwide. But I feel that God is using Prison Fellowship to bring his light and truth into the dark 'Hell-Holes' of prisons in our own country and throughout the world.

* * * * *

Part two - Marion's story
Unlike Derek, I was not brought up in a Christian home, but somehow I was 'God-conscious' from a very early age. Converted to Christ at fifteen, I went on to do all the normal things - I studied, worked, married and had a family.

But in my mid-thirties it seemed as if the Lord was

saying: 'Right, my lady, you've pretty well done your own thing up 'til now. There are a few matters that need sorting out here.'

By this time we had four children and my semi-invalid mother living with us. The pressures of life gradually increased until it was all too apparent that I was far from being the nice, even-tempered, patient woman I had imagined myself to be. I felt trapped by my circumstances. The harder I struggled to be free, the tighter I was gripped. The 'silent scream' became all too familiar, and I did what so many do; I looked for someone to blame. (Well, it couldn't be my fault, could it?) Sadly I focused all my bitterness and resentment on my mother.

Even now, ten years after her death, and with those feelings long since recognised to be groundless, and released, I am still ashamed to confess them. As I fell apart inside, the Lord unrelentingly obliged me to see myself in all my selfishness and inadequacy. I began to feel a tremendous urge not just to 'do' good, but to 'be' good. I kept thinking of Jesus' words in Matthew 5: 'Blessed are those who hunger and thirst for righteousness, for they shall be filled.' I was feeling anything but 'blessed'!

The day finally came when I gave in, admitted I could never 'be good' under my own steam, and asked the Lord to give me what I lacked.

His answer came at once as I remembered a verse from the Bible: 'God made him [Christ] who had no sin, to be sin for us, so that in him we might become the righteousness of God.' The first part of that scripture had become real for me when I was fifteen. It took over twenty years for me to grasp the second part!

The circumstances at home didn't change, but from then on I was given peace of heart and the strength to live with what had previously seemed overwhelming.

As time went on I wondered how best I could serve the Lord, and my thinking became focused on prayer. My restricted circumstances prevented me from actually doing much myself, but surely I could pray for those who did?

Right on cue a friend invited me to join the Prayer Chain Ministry - a group of women who agree to pray in their homes for specific needs, national and individual, as they are requested.

The three years I was involved in the Prayer Chain did three things: it showed me I had no idea how to pray, to really intercede; it challenged me to learn; and it taught me all over again that our God hears and answers our prayers.

All of this was good training for being part of the Prison Fellowship Prayer Support Group for Greenock Prison. Initially, three of us who did not go in with the Fellowship group, met to pray while the other volunteers were with the prisoners. Men, who at first were only names to us, became our friends as we brought them and their families to the Lord in prayer. We also prayed for our Chaplains, Governors and staff, many of them by name.

Months later, it was a very moving experience for us to actually meet the prisoners for whom we had been praying. This happened at the first seminar held in Greenock. One incident especially stands out in my memory.

A man with close-cropped hair was eyeing me out of the corner of his eyes as I went over to speak to him. We had been praying that he would come, and he had, so I was beaming all over my face. The next day a lump came to my throat when Derek passed on the prisoner's thanks for being so nice to him. But I had made no special effort - I had just been delighted that our prayers had been answered and he was there!

After meeting the men, we prayed with renewed fervour, for now the names were real people with real faces. One of the prisoners volunteered to gather and write down prayer requests from the men, and in return we gave him our prayer requests from outside. This idea came from men who, only months before, had been written off as 'no-hopers'.

As time went on we were privileged to see their thinking and attitudes changing; to see their pleasure in meeting with the Prison Fellowship team each week; to notice the many kindnesses they showed volunteers - such as the cards and scrolls they lovingly painted in the solitude of their cells. It was wonderful to find them eager to show their appreciation of the faithfulness of those who met with them each Wednesday and Sunday. Love begets love. As the fact of God's love for them began to filter through, they became free to respond in loving ways themselves.

Then the bombshell fell. 'Our men' were to go to other establishments, mainly the new prison at Shotts. They were to be replaced by Young Offenders serving long sentences.

That didn't seem like a fair deal to me, and I regret to say I told the Lord so in no uncertain terms! Not that it bothered him at all for, although I didn't know it, he was planning to 'sort me out' yet again!

A remark by one of our prisoners set the ball rolling. He mentioned 'uncaring people' making decisions for them. Naturally the men were not too happy at the prospect of moving, and his comment reinforced my smug feeling that 'those uncaring people' and I must be poles apart! Of course, my Father in heaven couldn't let me get away with that!

So for the next two weeks the Holy Spirit took me back step by step over the years that Derek had worked in prisons. With scorching power he brought to mind the times when I could have cared for prisoners and did not; times when I did care, but not enough. In short, the Holy Spirit revealed the almost total lack of real 'Christ love' in me.

Painful as these two weeks were, once I had truly repented I found myself somehow different. It is very hard to put into words. It was as though I had been jolted into alignment and thus was energised to do the work of Prison Fellowship, or indeed anything for those in prison. I now find that it is actually easier to do it, than not to do it. It was a faint echo of the Apostle Paul's words: 'Woe is me if I preach not the gospel.'

Looking back, it is clear that at least some experiences were preparation for involvement with Prison Fellowship - experiences which made it possible to relate, at least in part, to those we meet in prison. Confinement always brings pain, especially for those doing long sentences - the pain of loss of personal freedom, of separation from loved family and friends, of loss of control of one's life, of guilt and remorse at times. Both young and old experience this pain.

A teenager wrote the following lines when he was beginning a long sentence, and was suicidal over the suffering caused to his family by his trial and sentence:

Though I am dead, grieve not for me with tears.
Think not of death with sorrowing and fears.
I am so near that every tear you shed
Touches and tortures me, though you think me dead.
But when you laugh and sing with glad delight,
My soul is lifted upward to the light.
Laugh and be glad for all that life is giving,
And I, though dead, will share your joy in living.

Mercifully, his attempt to take his life was unsuccessful, but for many, imprisonment is literally a living death.

The last ten years hold many memories: sad ones; joyful ones; others that make us smile - like one inmate who was overheard extolling the virtues of our prison to a newcomer at the Fellowship. 'It's great, ye know. Ye get the peace'n quiet in yer 'peter'. Naebody tae bother ye. The grub's no' bad and no' only that, it's dead holy in here!'

Other memories are of weddings, baptisms, and sadly, of funerals. One was of a young man who died by his own hand. His family's grief was terrible to see. The faces of those Young Offenders who attended the Fellowship here come to mind frequently - four of them died before reaching their twenties. When we first met them, those same boys were brash, unmannerly, and frankly not easy to like, let alone love. Yet the Lord drew us all together to such an extent that we thought our hearts would break when they were moved on. One or two of them even shed tears! 'Who was it who changed?' I asked myself. 'Them or us?'

We recall individuals too - young women from Cornton Vale days whom we sometimes meet again at Prison Fellowship gatherings and who are still going on with the Lord; the man who, when others were trying to set the prison on fire outside the locked door of his cell, got through the ordeal by holding on to the Word of God which said: 'Do not be anxious ... the peace of God will keep your heart and mind...'; a young man who struggled to look any of us in the eye when we first met, but who put his trust in the Lord and when I last saw him, his face was literally shining. Such memories make us very thankful to God.

Sometimes a sceptic will ask: 'What do you get out of it?' The answer to this comes straight from the Bible: 'Good measure, pressed down, shaken together and running over.' To my shame, there was a time when the notion of my decent, respectable Christian self receiving anything from anyone in prison would have made my eyebrows climb. Now I am, I hope, humbled and wiser.

It would be impossible to tell here all that we have 'got out of it', but a few things stand out: the supreme joy of seeing some emerge from darkness into light; the love which grows where there is real sharing, not just with the prisoners, but with the other Prison Fellowship volunteers; the tremendous challenge and encouragement as we witness the faithfulness of those alongside whom we are privileged to work; the deepening of our own personal faith as the need to communicate the gospel sends us back to square one, to re-think what we ourselves truly believe; the 'hiding of God's Word in our hearts' as a necessary protection against being overwhelmed by worldly philosophy; the self-knowledge, often blisteringly painful, which springs from the examination of one's own thoughts and emotions in the need to relate to others; above all, the ever-increasing certainty of God's great love and faithfulness, especially when we least deserve it.

Being part of Prison Fellowship has been, and will continue to be, a learning process: learning humility, that without him we can do nothing; that we do not have answers for every question, and that it is far better to say so than to 'waffle'; learning not to hurt when even those nearest and dearest to us misunderstand what we do, or our motives in doing it; learning not to despair when those we long to see become Christians reject not only us, but Christ himself.

There are other things we must learn too: that it is not the end when we fall flat on our faces, if we have the guts to get up and begin again; that we must pray without ceasing, and never, but NEVER, give up on anyone; that we must not judge when reading newspaper reports of crime, which colour our thoughts and feelings about those we meet in prison; that we must keep always in our minds and prayers, the victims of crime; that we must give place graciously to someone else better equipped to do the task in hand, all the more so when we cannot see that he or she *is* better equipped; to be on guard when things are going well; to put on all God's armour and make full use of the 'sword of the Spirit', the Word of God.

Sharing Christ in prisons is not simply 'a good thing to do'. It is a real battle. Derek described prisons as 'Hell-holes', strongholds of Satan. Through the mighty working of God's Spirit, along with believing, persevering prayer, this is changing, and many inmates are being 'redeemed from the hand of the foe'.

* * * * *

To find out more about Gateside from an inmate's point of view, read Bill Varey's story which follows...

> 'Before this faith came, we were held prisoners by
> the law, locked up until faith should be revealed'
> (Galatians 3:23).

13

IN AND OUT OF LIFE'S
DARKEST RECESSES
by William 'Bill' Varey,
Inmate

It's 'Lock-up' Saturday afternoon as I sit and reflect on
the past two years as a Christian. The first thing that I
praise Jesus for is that it's no longer 'Lock Down' in the
Inverness 'Cages', where I spent six years for escape
attempts. While I was there I accumulated an extra
nineteen years to my sentence, bringing it to a total of
thirty-three years. My original sentence had been fourteen years for robbing a bank.

It was on my third visit to the Inverness Special Unit,
otherwise known as 'The Cages', that our Lord Jesus
Christ spoke to me. From then on his presence sustained
me for what was to come.

My back was giving me severe pain from an injury
sustained when jumping the Gatehouse of Peterhead
Prison on a bid for freedom, but now I was planning to
escape from 'The Unit' and had concealed a weapon
inside my radio. I kept the radio in the back Staff Room
- I was allowed to go there from time to time, ostensibly
to see if my radio was still working.

Then, early one morning, I was awakened by hearing one word: 'Forgive'.

Immediately I felt a deep sense of calm come over me. I had experienced this calm before in the cages, but this time there was also the word: Forgive. I knew instinctively that it was Jesus who had spoken it.

I had prayed to God many times before, but this time I got down on my knees and prayed as never before.

In the past I had listened to Dick Saunders on Radio Monte Carlo when he spoke on the Second Coming of Jesus. In these broadcasts Dick Saunders said that anyone who wanted to be saved should pray to God, confess his sins, and ask for forgiveness through Jesus. This is exactly what I did. But after the prayer I sensed an uneasy, nagging feeling about my escape plan and my weapon. I tried to put it out of my mind.

Shortly after that incident a Christian family first wrote and then visited me. They gave me a Bible and a small *Daily Light* book of Bible verses. After this my 'solitary' became solitude. I fed on the Word of God.

God spoke to me a second time. This time it was with the words: 'In and out of life's darkest recesses'.

I used to pray every day and thank him for sustaining me, but afterwards I always had the same sick feeling - as if I had the flu - and I was reminded of my weapon.

One morning as I was washing and shaving I decided to give the weapon to the Senior Officer. But somehow, it wasn't an easy thing to do. Every time I approached him to hand the weapon in, I found myself picking an argument with him instead. In the end after three attempts, I finally did hand the weapon to the Senior Officer working the afternoon shift.

He thanked me. I told him to thank Jesus. He looked at me suspiciously, then locked the door smartly behind him!

I did a dance of joy! The flu feeling had disappeared and that beautiful calm came upon me once again.

That comment, 'Thank Jesus', brought six psychiatrists to visit me in one day! They came into my 'Cage Area' in twos - it was like Noah's Ark!

The first couple asked: 'Hearing voices, are we, Mr. Varey?'

'Yes,' I replied.

'Who do you think it is?'

I laughed and told them, 'Jesus.'

'Hmm. Do you think you have a calling, Mr. Varey?'

I answered that our Lord had called worse than me for his purposes. I told them about Saul, who became Paul, who had been present at the stoning of Stephen and was on the road to Damascus to persecute Christians when he was converted. I must have passed their test because they didn't send me to Carstairs, Scotland's home for the criminally insane.

Twelve months later, when I was really concerned about what was going to happen to me, the Lord spoke to me again. This time it happened just as I was waking up.

'Bill,' the voice said.

I waited to see if there was more, but there was only the one word: Bill.

I really thought I had imagined it until I opened my *Daily Light* reading for the day, 26th November. There I read: 'For the Lord will take delight in you'; and just below that were the words: 'Fear not, for I have called you by name; you are mine.'

131

I felt a great joy knowing that the Lord had not only spoken a third time to me, but had confirmed it by his Word also.

After fourteen months I was moved to Greenock Prison. I arrived on 10th January, 1991. It is now the 4th of January, 1992 - my 43rd birthday - as I sit and write this. What a contrast the past year has been to my first six and a half years in prison! In fact, what a contrast the past two years have been to all the first forty! It is nothing short of a miracle.

I am now working, and I can have 'association' with other prisoners and join in physical education and other classes. I can attend the church service each Sunday. I can also go to the Prison Fellowship meeting every Wednesday. These meetings are run by Senior Officers, Derek Watt and Ian Lynch, and other Christian brothers and sisters. Derek's wife, Marion, runs the prayer support group which backs the prison in prayer.

Fellowship here in Greenock gives us the chance to share the Good News and encourage and strengthen one another through the Bible. God's Word really is 'living and active, sharper than any double-edged sword'. It is only through his Word that we can reach out to others who are still living in an atheistic, materialistic world.

I used to say, and hear others say, that being a Christian isn't easy. The only time it wasn't easy for me to be a Christian was when I looked to the world I knew instead of looking to the kingdom of God. In his letter to the Colossians, Paul tells us to 'set our hearts on things above where Christ is seated at the right hand of God'. And he's right. It's when we set our hearts on earthly things that living as a Christian is difficult. God's Word 'judges the thoughts and attitudes of the heart' and keeps us on the right track.

Today it is far easier for me to be a Christian. I have found a love that I cannot describe in any other way than spiritual. It fills my life. It is complete. At the Prison Fellowship meetings we try to share this love. A lot of men in prison have been hurt by 'love', but this is not the same kind of love. This is Christ's love as he showed it in his life and in his death.

Prison Fellowship gives us a chance to encourage men to know God through Jesus Christ and to help them take their first steps as children of God. Like all children, we all take our first steps differently. Some step out boldly; others wobble. But we all belong to a family, and there is always somebody to pick us up when we fall.

That is what Prison Fellowship is to me - a family, caring and sharing with the greatest Father of all, who loved us so much that he gave his one and only Son to die for us.

I was in one of life's darkest recesses. Only such a love could have brought me out.

* * * * *

We switch now to Low Moss Prison to hear a Social Worker describe his involvement - and his worldwide travels for Prison Fellowship.

> 'You brought us into prison and laid burdens on our backs. You let men ride over our heads; we went through fire and water, but you brought us to a place of abundance' (Psalm 66:11,12).

14

TO BARLINNIE AND BEYOND
by Angus Creighton,
Social Worker, H.M. Prison, Low Moss

Travelling along the M8 motorway in Glasgow, near Junction 12, you first catch sight of the tall chimneys and long halls of Barlinnie, a few hundred metres away. Alias 'The Bar-L' or the 'Big House', Barlinnie has been part of the Glasgow scene ever since it opened its gates in 1882.

I well remember my first day there. It was August, 1979, and I only survived by being able to escape briefly around mid-day in order to recapture my sense of freedom. I never thought that, as the new Senior Social Worker in the prison, I was starting an eight year 'stretch', or that Barlinnie would become 'a place of abundance' to me.

I soon met Tom Flannery and Ian Lynch, both Prison Officers and fellow Christians. Tom was a Catholic and Ian an Episcopalian, but they regularly got together in each other's homes to read the Bible and pray. I was delighted when they invited me, a Baptist, to join them.

In February 1980 another Senior Social Worker came to Barlinnie. Ian Reid was a nominal Christian and we used to have some great debates about Christianity during lunch. I had just finished reading Chuck Colson's latest book *Life Sentence*, and Ian said he would like to read it too. It was through reading that book that Ian committed his life to Christ and joined our small staff group.

Soon afterwards Dr. Duncan Neil, another Baptist, came to Barlinnie. He had applied for a vacancy in the prison hospital a year earlier, but had been unsuccessful. When the post became vacant again, Duncan had been asked if he was still interested. He had been praying for guidance and took this to be God's will that he should accept the position as Prison Doctor. We gladly welcomed him into our staff group. What, we wondered, was God planning to do in Barlinnie?

There was already a Sunday afternoon Bible Class led by Gordon Haxton and Ian Gilfillan, and Father 'Ned' Lindsay and Rev David Hogg, the Roman Catholic and Church of Scotland Chaplains, also had a high profile around the prison. As a staff group we supported all these people but, as we all worked varying shift patterns, we were unable to be actively involved in the spiritual life of the prison in an official way.

When we became aware of the work of Prison Fellowship in the United States, we wrote asking for more information, and shortly afterwards I was invited to attend a meeting at Louise Purvis' home. There I became part of the original Prison Fellowship Scotland 'core group'.

I reported back to our staff group at the prison and we decided to ask the Governor and Chaplains if we could start to meet 'inside'. They gave us permission to use the

Chaplain's room in the main administration block and we continued to meet and pray together there for several months, forging strong bonds of fellowship in spite of our different roles in prison, our denominational differences and our varying expressions of worship.

Some time later an ex-terrorist from Prison Fellowship Northern Ireland came to visit us and we invited him for a meal. He told us that in Northern Ireland, such an expression of Christian fellowship would be extremely dangerous for prison staff. He was amazed and deeply moved by the diversity and unity of our small group.

Around the middle of November 1981 Chuck Colson visited Scotland to launch Prison Fellowship officially, and Barlinnie was one of the places he visited. The day he came, the Governor had delegated the Senior Chaplain, David Hogg, who had earlier been co-opted to our core group, to escort the party around the prison.

It was dull and cloudy as we walked around the work sheds and some of the halls. But when we reached 'B' hall, where Tom Flannery was on duty, a shaft of sunlight suddenly streamed through the hall and lit up the spot where Chuck Colson and Tom were standing. To me, it seemed like a symbol of things to come.

Then the Governor joined us and took over. Towards the end of the tour, having discovered that Chuck Colson was an ex-marine like himself, the Governor invited him and the rest of the party to tea in the Boardroom. This gesture did a great deal to smooth away the misgivings which some staff had felt. One member of staff had declared that 'Chuck Colson was just a flash-in-the-pan Yank', while others thought that Prison Fellowship had CIA links because of Chuck Colson!

After Chuck's visit we continued to meet and pray together for several months and eventually felt we should approach the Governor and Chaplains for permission to open up our group to include the prisoners. I'm not sure what I expected but, although the Governor did grant permission, he surprised me by stipulating that the group should be a 'closed' in-prison group, solely between staff and prisoners.

I knew that the prison Bible Class often brought in 'outsiders' to speak and take part. I also knew that the 'open' pattern existed in other prisons such as Dungavel, where their 'Friday group' had been going into the prison for some time.

But at least we had permission. What we needed next was a place to meet. We could no longer use the Chaplain's office for security reasons. Neither was the prison Chapel a suitable venue. Then David Clark, another officer who had joined the group, had the vision of a 'White House' at the centre of Barlinnie as a place where we should meet.

This turned out to be the Social Work unit where Ian and I worked! It had a large carpeted room with a toilet and kitchen adjacent, and enough comfortable chairs to enable us to sit in a circle. Our Social Work colleagues kindly agreed to let us use the room, and necessary arrangements were made to cover the security and escort requirements.

Thursday evenings, between 6.30 and 7.45, were chosen as the most suitable time. One reason for that choice was that on Thursday evenings 'Top of the Pops' was on television. The men who came to the Fellowship would have to make a conscious choice to join us!

Another reason was that we now had a prayer support group outside the prison which met on the third Thursday of the month to pray for us and Low Moss Prison. We thought that, as members of that prayer group were not allowed into Barlinnie, prison staff members could go along to their prayer group afterwards and give them news and prayer topics and tell them of any answered prayers. Ex-prisoners quite often came along to the prayer support group and we had many glorious evenings of prayer, praise and fellowship at Royal Exchange Square. The wives of the prison staff who lived near to the prison also formed themselves into a prayer group and met twice a week in different homes.

The pattern of our fellowship meetings both inside and outside the prison was basically the same. After introductions and some singing we had prayer, fellowship and Bible study. This helped the prisoners to feel at home whether inside or outside the prison. It also prepared them for our ultimate goal - to see them integrated into a caring local church of their particular denomination.

The first staff/prisoners' group at Barlinnie opened with five long-term prisoners who had shown an interest. It took a lot of 'bottle', or courage, for them to join what, until then, had been a staff group. However, they were committed to following Christ, and their lives had an impact on the rest of the prison population. Later, other prisoners joined the group out of interest, and our numbers grew.

Many men sensed an atmosphere of safety within the fellowship and felt strangely at ease in the room. We knew that this was due to the Lord being with us.

Eventually many of the men came to an awareness of their need to repent and believe in Christ.

After a while some group traditions developed. For instance, we addressed each other by our Christian names. Also, on the Thursday before a prisoner's release, we presented him with a 'Good News' New Testament which we had all signed. These became precious possessions to many of the men. Some even came back with their Testaments - on subsequent sentences!

We found that a great bond of caring and concern developed between us, especially when prisoners began to pray for each other, for their families, friends and staff. This made it possible to maintain yet another custom. At the end of each Fellowship meeting, we stood and said the Lord's Prayer together, holding hands in a circle. This was an unusual practice in a prison, but it was an expression of real Christian fellowship between staff and inmates.

We always tried to choose meaningful hymns and choruses, and one favourite became known as the 'Barlinnie Special': 'Father, I place into your hands the things that I can't do...'

When our group was growing quite large, we asked the prisoners if they would like to split into two groups - one for the more fully committed and another for those who were just 'interested'. They decided unanimously to stay as one group.

The differences we saw in the lives of the prisoner members as a result of studying the Bible were quite marked. One member, Eddie, had a fearsome reputation for violence towards inmates as well as staff. The change in Eddie's life was a gradual one, but staff throughout the prison noticed and respected him for it. On the day of his release, Eddie handed me a bunch of stolen car keys as evidence that the Lord is interested in crime prevention!

Another prisoner, Andy, was released one morning and was back at night. I saw him in reception and asked what had happened. Without telling anyone what he was going to do, he had gone to his lawyer and changed his plea on an outstanding charge from 'not guilty' to 'guilty'. His amazed lawyer had him dealt with immediately in court and he was returned to Barlinnie on remand. As a consequence a group of men in his untried hall asked for a Prison Fellowship group! A Catholic and a Church of Scotland Chaplain teamed up and ran the group during the day.

Eventually the evening Prison Fellowship group became too large. About thirty men, including a number of men on 'protection', were attending. Normally it was not allowed for men on 'protection' to mix with the rest of the prison population, but such was the degree of trust which the staff placed on the fellowship group that they permitted this. No untoward incident ever occurred with these men.

As a staff group we prayed together before each meeting, asking God's blessing and mentioning specific issues. The way God answered our prayers about the overcrowding came as a surprise to us all.

First Ian Lynch was sent as part of an advance party of staff to Gateside Prison, Greenock, which was being refurbished. Later, some of our committed prisoner members were also sent there, which further reduced our numbers. The first group of these men to enter their hall at Gateside found that Ian Lynch was on duty there! It really made the transition easier for both prisoners and staff. (You will already have read what developed there in Chapter Twelve.) So, with our overcrowding problems solved, we waited for the numbers to pick up again. By this time Prison Fellowship was well-known in the prison, so when it was time to round up the members, the hall staff used to call out loudly: 'Send down the God Squad!'

As Social Workers and members of Prison Fellowship, Ian Reid and I had to try to ensure that we kept each of these roles separate. This was difficult at times, especially when prisoners in the Fellowship asked to see us urgently in our roles as Social Workers, during or after the Fellowship meeting. Some expected to be treated differently from the rest of the prisoners, and we needed wisdom from God. Occasionally we did have disgruntled prisoners but we referred them to the Chaplains, as our relations with them were good. When one prisoner in the Fellowship asked to be baptised, the Chaplains were delighted to oblige.

Ian later felt God's call to the Church of Scotland ministry and is now a minister in the Isle of Skye. In his Barlinnie days he felt he had seen the 'fleshing out' of what he had read in *Life Sentence*, where ex-Black Panther and Ku Klux Klan members had come together in Christ. He felt the same thing had been re-enacted in the Barlinnie fellowship group between Catholics and Protestants, prisoners and staff. The fellowship we shared across our various denominations opened his eyes to the dynamic of the gospel.

The Fellowship team emphasised the need to attend Sunday services and the Bible class. On one occasion we invited the Chaplains and Bible Class leaders to join us for a day's seminar which the Christian volunteers from outside were also able to attend. From time to time we hosted 'Gospel Concerts', with Prison Fellowship speakers and musical contributions from lively, young Christian groups. At Christmas it became a tradition to show the Johnny Cash video *The Gospel Road*, and afterwards we enjoyed home-made Christmas mince pies!

Sometimes prisoners wanted deeper Bible teaching and we referred them to the Chaplains. When one wished to study New Testament Greek, the Fellowship gave him his text book.

Towards the end of 1986 the work had outgrown Louise Purvis' part-time role as Co-ordinator, and Prison Fellowship began to look for a full-time paid Director. One morning Colin Cuthbert, a drugs worker with the Possil Drugs Project, came to Barlinnie to interview a prisoner. Colin asked to see me afterwards and in conversation I mentioned Prison Fellowship's need for a Director. After prayer and discussion with his wife, May, and having received several other promptings, Colin applied for the post and became our executive Director at the beginning of February 1987. (For more on this story, see Chapter 17.)

In January 1987 Barlinnie became the scene of a serious riot. Tom Flannery was briefly held hostage and David Clark was injured in a separate incident. The Fellowship group was cancelled for some time. What really moved the team was the great concern of the prisoner members for the Fellowship staff. They prayed for us and eventually the Fellowship recommenced. The deep bonds between us partly made up for the loss and destruction many had experienced.

Towards the middle of 1987 I left Barlinnie, exchanging posts with Helena Bryce, a Senior Social Work colleague at Low Moss Prison. Helena had been a part of Prison Fellowship since the first meeting at Louise Purvis' home. Ironically she brought new ideas with her from the Greenock Fellowship which had once been influenced by Ian Lynch from the Barlinnie Fellowship! This cross-fertilisation of ideas has been one of the richnesses of Prison Fellowship as inmates and staff have moved around in the prison system. [1]

* * * * *

1. Helena briefly brings the story of Barlinnie Fellowship up to date.

'When I came from Greenock Prison to Barlinnie, I had to make the adjustment from working with long-term to short-term prisoners. This meant that many of the men moved quickly through the Fellowship and I didn't have the same time to build up a real depth of friendship. This helped me realise the need to make the gospel message clear at each meeting, without losing the feeling of fellowship. I appreciated coming into an established group with a definite place in the prison programme as well as the support of prison management and the Chaplain's team.

This has allowed us to move from being a 'closed' staff group to an open group, with some members of the Glasgow Prayer Support group now joining us. There is no doubt that having our 'own' officer, William Hunter, with us each week has made a huge difference. His enthusiasm for the group has increased the numbers of men attending and created a pool of officers willing to take part in his absence. The Lord has really blessed the group and we have seen many lives changed. The vision of 'one prisoner telling another' has been fulfilled many times. It is now very much the inmates' Fellowship, and they will not allow anyone to jeopardise its future by unacceptable behaviour.

We give God the glory for the past ten years and look forward with great anticipation to what he is going to do in the future.'

In June 1982 I started travelling far beyond the bounds of Barlinnie. I represented Prison Fellowship Scotland at Rostrevor in Northern Ireland where I met representatives of Prison Fellowship from England and Wales, Northern Ireland, The Irish Republic and Canada. This was the forerunner of an annual get-together of the Chairmen and Directors of the European Prison Fellowships. Fifteen countries, including the then Soviet Union, and a number of Eastern European countries were represented in Malta in March, 1991.

In July 1983 the First International Convocation of Prison Fellowship was held in Belfast. By this time Prison Fellowship Scotland was a chartered member of the International Fellowship and many of us attended. The theme was 'In Christ ... Reconciliation', and two ex-terrorists, from opposite sides of the community divide, were paroled in order to attend the convocation. It was moving to see them speaking together from the platform as brothers in Christ, when they had once been trying to kill each other.

In the autumn of 1983 I was asked to represent Prison Fellowship International at a Spanish Prison Ministry Conference in Madrid. A growing number of evangelicals had caught the vision of reaching all Spanish prisons with the gospel, and they were well on the way to their goal. When I returned for the 1987 Conference it was wonderful to see how their work had progressed and to encourage them by relating what God was doing around the world through Prison Fellowship.

In 1987 the Prison Fellowship office at the Christian Centre in Bishopbriggs was opened. It was quite close to Low Moss Prison where I was working, so the new

Director, Colin Cuthbert, and I were able to meet there regularly at lunch times. After I was elected Chairman in November 1987 we also went away for the occasional day of prayer, fellowship and discussion together. In June 1989 we represented Prison Fellowship Scotland at the Third Prison Fellowship International Convocation in San Jose, Costa Rica, where more than 250 participants from 58 countries attended. For Colin and me some of the highlights were the early morning prayer meetings when we heard from some wonderful Christians from around the world. Many of them were ex-prisoners like Irina Ratushinskaya, the Russian dissident poet and Father Lawrence Jenco, the ex-hostage in Lebanon.

To our great surprise, Prison Fellowship Scotland was presented with an award of excellence which read: 'In recognition of their impact on society, through the development of an exemplary model of participation among all the churches in their community.' The credit for this award, humanly speaking, must go to the hundreds of volunteers and the unnumbered prayer supporters of the Fellowship throughout Scotland.

Costa Rica will always be special to me for two reasons. First it meant a return to the continent of my birth, and second I was elected to the Board of Prison Fellowship International. I was replacing Sylvia Mary Alison of England and Wales, who had been such a great inspiration to us in beginning Prison Fellowship in Scotland. I felt deeply honoured to become one of the two European representatives.

July 1990 was memorable for Prison Fellowship International. I was invited to attend the First National Prison Conference in the Soviet Union, with Ron Nikkel,

Prison Fellowship International's President. Participants at the conference represented on-going ministry in more than 200 prisons, and this was taking place when the prisons had only been open to Christians for less than a year! Some of those attending had been imprisoned for their faith, and others for criminal offences. Delegates from many different Christian denominations and from eleven of the fifteen republics attended.

Ron and I were overwhelmed by the reception we received. The singing, the prayers and the warm, loving fellowship were unforgettable. We had been invited to encourage and inform them about the International Prison Fellowship scene. They, in turn, were a great inspiration to us. They appointed a committee to continue working together and we pray the day will come when they become part of the International Family of Prison Fellowship.

With the tenth anniversary of our own Fellowship in Scotland in the autumn of 1991, the International Board of Prison Fellowship was scheduled to meet in Scotland too. We were thrilled to have Chuck Colson with us and many of the International Board members spoke movingly in Scottish churches and prisons about the work of Prison Fellowship in India, Kenya, Germany, Australia, the USA, Brazil, Norway, El Salvador, the Ivory Coast, Iceland, England and Wales and Northern Ireland.

We were inspired by the faithfulness of volunteers like Johann and Lara Gudmundsson, who have been ministering alone for years in Iceland. We heard with astonishment about thousands of inmates being freed in one day in El Salvador, because a Prison Fellowship lawyer had found a loop-hole in the law. We were incredulous when we heard of the 'prison without guards' in Brazil being run by three Prison Fellowship leaders and the inmates! As the repeat offender's rate in that prison has dropped from 86 per cent to 6 per cent, prison authorities around the world have begun to watch and copy their model.

* * * * *

I went back to Barlinnie some time ago. Many new volunteers have joined the Fellowship but of the original team, only Dr. Duncan Neil remains. Here are some of the thoughts he shared with me.

'I was attracted to Prison Fellowship because it rose above the barriers of denomination ... It brought men and women together and united them in a love for our Lord which was then radiated to men and women in prison.

'I contended that, along with better management and a more caring attitude, Prison Fellowship would help to make Barlinnie Prison a better place in which to work and, more importantly, would give men an opportunity to begin again and find a much more meaningful and fulfilled life. I think it has achieved this.'

Some of our prisoner brothers are still 'inside' and involved in the Prison Fellowship groups all over Scotland. Others are out of prison, attending local churches and they keep in touch by letter. Other ex-prisoners go back into prison as part of our Prison Fellowship teams. We can all be encouraged by the truth that God is faithful. It was the Psalmist who said: 'You brought us into prison and laid burdens on our backs. You let men ride over our heads; we went through fire and water, but you brought us to a place of abundance.'

* * * * *

Ex-inmate Joe Connelly also spent some time in Barlinnie, among other places and he gives us his angle on it in Chapter Sixteen. But first let's hear from 32 year old Calum who has served seven years of a life sentence in Peterhead ...

> 'I was in prison and you came to visit me.' Then the righteous will answer him, 'Lord, when did we see you ... sick or in prison and go to visit you?' The King will reply, 'I tell you the truth, whatever you did for one of the least of these brothers of mine, you did for me' (Matthew 25:36-40).

15

GOD'S UNEXPECTED VISITORS
by Malcolm 'Calum' Mackay,
Inmate

As a child on the Isle of Lewis I liked being out in the open air, playing football, fishing and other things like that. I remember wanting to be a fireman when I grew up.

I went to Sunday School and church and I liked the Bible stories they told us, even though I didn't really understand them. Later on I drifted away from Sunday School, and on Sundays I went for walks down by the seashore instead.

I had a nice home and good parents - but that didn't stop me from getting into trouble. And when I got into trouble at school it meant more rows at home. At first it was little things - not doing as I was told, not listening to the teacher, talking back or breaking windows. Maybe I was just trying to get attention.

As I got older the little things became more serious things. I started to steal from shops and other places. Sometimes I was caught and then the police would be involved and there would be more rows with my parents. I know now that they meant well, but at the time I could not cope with their rebukes, and I rebelled even more.

In school I did learn a bit, though I was only interested in certain subjects. I liked woodwork and technical drawing, but not writing and spelling. I'd have liked to do cookery, but that was only for girls. The teachers had their troubles with me; I was disruptive in class - or else I fell asleep! Once I even set off the fire extinguisher!

I left school at sixteen with no qualifications and went to work as an apprentice baker. After about six months there I went to work on the fishing boats for the next five years. At the same time I started to drink and it soon became a drug to me. I was a pretty wild character at that stage, and I certainly didn't want to settle down.

The fishing is a great way of life - hard, cold and wet at times, but great all the same. The schedule depends on what kind of boat you're on and what kind of fish you're working. You can be at sea for the working week and have the weekend off, or you can have a month at sea and a week off. But whatever schedule I was on, I'd head for the nearest bar as soon as I got ashore, and that would be me drinking till it was time to sail again.

Sometimes, if I still had money, I'd let them sail without me and keep on drinking. Then I'd get onto another boat once the money ran out. I was asked to leave some of the boats, but I'd just get onto another, until they too had had enough of my drinking and asked me to go. How I didn't cause loss of life among the fishermen working with me, or how I wasn't lost at sea myself, I'll never know. I can only believe that even then, God was looking after me, and the men with me, keeping us safe.

When I came ashore I didn't go home. Instead I stayed in the Fishermen's Mission rather than go to my parents and face any rows about my habits. When I stayed in the Mission I'd come in drunk at night and in the morning I'd be back out to drink again.

At that point I'd been picked up by the Police a few times for drinking, but I'd never been in prison - though I was once held overnight in the Police station. But then, one afternoon when I was drunk, I was arrested for assault and started to fight with the policemen. I was sent to prison and after three months in the untried wing, I was given twenty-seven months. I served seven months and was released on parole.

That prison term did make me think a little. I was sorry for what I had done wrong, and I could see that drinking was not helping me. I didn't really enjoy my way of life - or being in prison. In fact, I could see I was in a mess. How much of a mess I was soon to learn.

When I was given parole I went to stay in a 'dry house' for alcoholics and I managed to stay off drink for about six months. Then I went to work in a hotel. I enjoyed the work, but I started to drink again and was asked to leave. I moved out into a Bed and Breakfast place in Edinburgh, and over the following year I drank a lot and started taking drugs.

I had a girlfriend, but one day when she went home to see her family, I got drunk and ended up killing a woman who was staying in the same Bed and Breakfast house. I handed myself over to the Police and was given a life sentence. I was sent to Peterhead Prison.

Murder is not easily explained - nor are the thoughts before or after. I can only say that I am truly sorry, although I know that does not help much.

But for me, a life sentence, as well as being an end, was to be a beginning. Not just the beginning of a new life inside prison but a new beginning inside myself. This was partly due to circumstances that I only discovered much later.

Unknown to me at that time, a Christian couple, Willie and Marion, were living a couple of doors down from the house where I'd committed the murder. They also came from the island of Lewis and they were both volunteers in Prison Fellowship.

On the day of the murder they had seen a group of us having 'a high old time' in the garden and later, cycling by, Willie had noticed police activity around the house and surrounding gardens. He soon learned that there had been a murder and that I, a fellow Lewisman, had been charged. Because of their involvement with Prison Fellowship and because I came from Lewis, they started to pray for me regularly. When my trial came up, Marion and a Christian friend attended it and prayed throughout.

After I was sentenced Willie found my address through the Prison Fellowship office and wrote to me in Gaelic, introducing himself as a neighbour in Edinburgh and a fellow 'Isleman' from Lewis. I sent a brief note back to him, and so started a relationship which continues to this day.

When I discovered that Willie and Marion had known me by sight and had seen me on the day of the murder, and still kept praying for me, I was moved. I was also moved that Marion and her friend should attend my trial and pray. (Willie later told me that he too would have been there except for his job as a headmaster.) Willie and

Marion still write to me faithfully and visit me from Lewis three times a year.

Soon after moving to Lewis from Edinburgh, Willie and Marion started a prayer support group on the island. It is attended by men, women and children and includes three ex-inmates, now newly committed Christians, and my mother. They all prayed that I would receive Jesus into my heart. Their prayers passed through prison walls and were God's first prison visitors to me.

My mother had been converted shortly before my crime, and she believes that the Lord was preparing her to face the terrible situation which was about to happen. I believe it was her prayers which helped to prepare my heart for change. She herself has been sustained by the prayers and support of the Lewis Prison Fellowship prayer group, and this in turn has brought great comfort to me.

But my life did not change overnight. I was still taking drugs, when I was able to get them, and was mentally in a mess. I was sorry for all the harm and heartache I had caused to so many people. Sometimes I was even sorry for having lived.

Then I started to read the Bible. I thought if I did this everything would come right overnight. But it seemed as if everything got worse rather than better! It was a while before I realised that God is in control and changes take time.

Sometimes my mind was in turmoil as God brought scenes from my past life to my mind - scenes which made me cringe. I felt ashamed and hurt and angry with myself for what I'd done and for what I'd become. Unfortunately I took my anger out on others, but it was the beginning of real repentance.

I kept reading more and more of the Bible. But you can't read the Bible for very long and still continue to do things like taking drugs. It is a book of power - God's power - and you will either put the Bible down or put aside the drugs. God helped me to put aside the drugs.

I began to see that Jesus is Lord and that he had brought me to this prison so that I could learn more about God and his wonders.

The first of these lessons occurred one night when I was sitting on my bed in the dark, feeling down. I was about three years into my sentence and, although I had been reading the Bible and praying, nothing seemed to be right. I was not coping with my life or the things inside me and really wanted to end it all. Everything was a mess and pointless. I could not even look out of the window, because I knew I'd see the fishing boats going out to sea and I'd feel a sad longing for the days I used to work on the boats.

As I sat there a thought came to my mind. 'Look out of the window.' I didn't want to, but again the thought came: 'Look out of the window.'

So I got up and opened the curtains and looked out. And as I looked, it was as if a curtain were being opened within my mind. I felt the dark thoughts leave me as I saw something I had only ever seen before on TV - a little baby owl sitting on the prison fence!

Nothing else seemed to matter at that moment as I looked with love and wonder at that small creature. He seemed to be looking in at me as if to say: 'Hello Calum. I'm here too.'

I wanted to wake up the whole prison and get everyone to look at the little baby owl which had been sent by the

Lord to comfort and cheer me. It may only have been a little owl, but to me it meant so much more - as if the Lord was showing me a little of his world that I couldn't see.

I still remember that incident with wonder. I was at the end. I couldn't see a way of going on, but the sight of the little baby owl reminded me of the Lord's comfort, hope, love and care for all his creatures.

First he had used prayers; then he had sent Willie and Marion; now this was God's third prison visitor. Netta was the fourth.

Netta is a Prison Fellowship volunteer who visits me and helps me cope with any problems. After one of her visits I was sitting on the bed, trying to write her a letter thanking her for her kindness in visiting me. As I wrote, I saw that by living her life in accordance with the Lord's will and Word, he was alive and living through her. As I realised that, I broke down and cried because of my love and gratitude.

And as I wept I knew that, although the Lord Jesus was put to death nearly two thousand years ago, he was alive and living through Netta, and I had been allowed to see a little of his light for a moment of time. I believe he is still alive today, in the twentieth century. He lives in Netta's letters and visits.

Another time I heard one of the wonders of the Lord. One day two Lutheran nuns visited us in the prison church. They had been invited by one of the Chaplains, now a Trustee of Prison Fellowship.

That day I was sitting two rows in front of the visitors but no one was immediately behind me or on my left. When they had told us about some of the Lord's work, we started to sing a hymn. As everyone was singing, I started to listen - and heard a beautiful voice singing beside my left ear. I felt as if I was hearing an angel of the Lord, singing praise. I could have listened to that voice singing forever. I know that it could only have been the voice of an angel singing in my ear, for it was more beautiful than the word 'beautiful' can explain. I felt this was another visitor from the Lord.

One night I was allowed to visit Prison Fellowship in another prison. After a few minutes general conversation, we sat in a circle to sing hymns. As I was sitting there, a question came into my mind: 'How are you feeling?'

I thought about it and knew that I was feeling really at home and at peace just sitting there quietly. There is something different and special about being together with God and his people.

One night God sent me another visitor. Here in Peterhead, every prisoner has a cell to himself, so after everyone is locked up for the night, each prisoner is alone in his cell. That night when I was falling asleep, I jumped up with a start, scared stiff. I could feel 'a warm person' sitting on my bed! Then my fear slowly subsided, and I wanted to cuddle up into the warmth. I knew it was another unexpected visitor from the Lord. Prison bars cannot keep him out!

I have now served seven years and am working on the eighth. It has not been easy at times. There have been some days and nights when I've had to think back to the night the Lord Jesus sent his owl, and an angel, and the prayers and letters and visits of his people as his visitors to me. I have to remember Jesus' help at those times and to remind myself that, even in the darkest times, he is with me.

The Lord Jesus has taught me a lot about myself. I know now that I have lived most of my life without thinking or caring about other people's feelings. I was wrong and I am sorry.

Mentally I am calmer than I was. My thoughts aren't so mixed up and I don't feel so mad at myself any more. I believe others are seeing the Lord Jesus working in my life. An officer told me a few months ago that when I first came here some men were afraid of me because of my anger. But they have noticed that I am calmer now. I know it is God who is making the changes.

The Lord has encouraged me to take up my education and, even though I still can't spell very well, he has enabled me to learn Braille and, through his grace, I have been able to transcribe some magazines into Braille. I am now transcribing a book.

I may not have explained things well, and some may wonder about some of my experiences, but I hope the Lord will help everyone to know that all I have written is true.

I hope and pray that you will find it in your hearts to pray that those in prison will find healing and peace and a new life in the Lord. I thank everyone who prayed for me and hope the Lord will bless them all.

It is a great joy to me that I am now a part of the Prison Fellowship prayer group which meets in Lewis. Although distance and prison walls separate us, 'nothing can separate us from the love of God', and prayer overcomes these obstacles. Perhaps my prayers will help now to bring others into God's kingdom, as other people's prayers brought me in. In that way my prayers can also become some of God's unexpected prison visitors.

* * * * *

Unlike Calum, our next contributor, Joe Connelly, thought he was in pretty good shape. He had friends, money, possessions - all the things that make the world go round. But it hadn't always been that way....

> 'But while he was still a long way off, his father saw him and was filled with compassion for him; he ran to his son, threw his arms around him and kissed him. The son said to him, "Father I have sinned against heaven and against you. I am no longer worthy to be called your son." But the father said, "... Let's have a feast and celebrate. For this son of mine was dead and is alive again; he was lost and is found" ' (Luke 15:19-24).

16

FROM god TO GOD
by Joe Connelly,
Ex-inmate

My father worked hard all his life, yet never had much to show for it. My mother used to speak about God and putting your trust in him. Yet, where was he?, I sometimes asked myself. Maybe somewhere deep down he was there, but the lure of another god had taken precedence in my mind - MONEY.

I saw it as the great solver of problems, the great healer of pain, the great provider. This god seemed more attractive to me. So I began a life of worship and adoration of him. 'Seek and you will find' - it wasn't hard. Lots of people had it. 'Ask and you will receive' - if you don't, you just take it. 'And the door will be opened to you' - if it wasn't, you just kicked it in. My god was a great god. He was everywhere - if you looked in the right places.

Yet deep down inside there was a nagging emptiness which I couldn't forget.

I learned early on that it was unwise to trust people - they can be a key to a door that can keep you from your freedom. But until then, what a freedom this god gives! He gives so much, and for a long time you can get away with it - as I did. Then, all of a sudden, BANG! It all catches up with you, and you find yourself in a cell. First in a Police Station, then in a Young Offenders' Institution. What an experience!

The first time this happened to me I went down on my knees crying, praying for forgiveness, making oaths never to do it again if I could just be freed. And my prayers were answered! I was remanded in custody for one week, then released on bail pending trial. Oh, the sweet taste of freedom! But of course, once out the pleas and the oaths faded into the never-never.

I went through this performance several times when I was a young man, and the outcome was always the same.

I served my first prison sentence in Aberdeen for stealing 35,000 cigarettes. Even then, I was lucky. The driver who took us to Aberdeen had 'done a runner' and if they'd caught him, we might have been convicted on a more serious charge of 'conspiracy', as travelling thieves. As it happened I got six months, backdated from my remand date.

I was still in prison at Christmas, 1982 - miles from home and locked up with all these guys with 'foreign', i.e. north-east of Scotland, accents. But I was lucky - you find Glaswegians in even the most remote prisons in Britain, so it wasn't long before I had made some friends of my own kind. They helped the time to pass. When you're serving a sentence it seems like an eternity but the day you walk out of the gate, it is as if it were no time at all.

The day I got out of Aberdeen I had to appear in Glasgow Sheriff Court on a deferred sentence for the theft of whisky from a warehouse. My lawyer told me that if the Sheriff didn't find out that I'd come out of Craiginches that morning, I'd be OK. But he did find out! Halfway through the hearing, a policeman came in and spoke to the Prosecutor, who told the Sheriff. I was sentenced to nine months imprisonment.

I had a great lawyer. While I was serving the nine months, he got all my outstanding charges brought together and I was given a total of thirty-three months added to my sentence. That was the bad news. The good news was that only nine of those were to run consecutively. The rest were to run concurrently.

Prison is a great college of crime. I went in a thief and came out with all the knowledge and contacts I needed to earn the big money in DRUGS. I remember watching one of my best friends waste away through heroin. I tried it once myself and 'spewed my ring'.

'Forget it if that's what it does,' I thought.

But one night at a party, I felt really left out so I took a 'line' of it. 'What have I been missing?' I thought.

It gave me a great feeling of confidence. I could say the things I wanted to say, do the things I wanted to do. My dreams and ambitions became greater.

Within a year I was 'freebasing' and at the end of four years I had smoked two businesses into bankruptcy. The balloon had burst. What was it all about? Money is the great illusion. Even when I had plenty, it didn't bring me

161

happiness. Now drugs had taken the money and left me with an addiction and a messed up life. But the greater mess was within.

At that point something happened which started me off in a new direction. Early in 1986 my older brother, David, asked me to go to a Christian Men's Breakfast. I had never been one for visiting family, so I thought I would go along to make up for not having visited either him or my other brothers and sisters.

My brother arranged to come and pick me up at 7.30 a.m. on the Saturday morning. I arrived home on Friday night with three grammes of cocaine. By 5.30 a.m. I was sitting like a space cadet. At 6.30 a.m. I had a bath to try and sort myself out. I put two large 'lines' on the fireplace. At 7.35 a.m. I could hear my brother coming up the stairs, so I took both 'lines' and shook myself. I was feeling good.

We arrived at the hotel to be welcomed by two fellows with grins on their faces from ear to ear. It was all new to me, all these guys shaking hands and hugging. Yet there was something I couldn't put my finger on. I went to these breakfasts on several occasions after that.

And it was at one of them that I met a larger than life fellow who seemed to look right into my soul. His name was Colin Cuthbert. I found I could not look him in the eye. He asked me some questions about myself, but I was a pro at answering. He intrigued me though. He gave me his 'phone number and address and said to contact him any time.

A few months later, everything started on a downward spiral. The brewers, the V.A.T. men and many more creditors were wanting money. How could I tell them I was smoking it faster than it was coming in?

It was at this point that I decided to contact the big fellow I had met at the Breakfast. He turned out to be the Director of Prison Fellowship Scotland and he invited me to come to his office. It was a meeting that would change my life.

We had lunch in a cafe and then went back to his office where we started chatting about things in general. Then something started to happen. When I spoke, it was as if I was listening to someone else talking. To this day I still cannot understand exactly what happened.

The only comparison I can make to it is the feeling you get when entering prison. First you sit in what's known as the 'dug box'. When the guards are ready, they bring you out to the reception area. Then they tell you to strip off. I have never felt so degraded - standing there naked with all the different people walking around. Next you have a shower and get kitted out with prison clothes. The experience made me feel totally vulnerable.

It was the same kind of feeling I had with Colin, except that my nakedness was inside. I knew I was being seen for who I really was. But the hardest part was that I felt it was me looking at me, from the outside in. In hindsight, I know the Lord stood there with me, telling me that he accepted me just as I was and that he could change it all. Maybe he believed it, but I ran away! I soon discovered though, that nothing would ever be the same for me again.

The thought of going into prison was very frightening to me at that time. Five years on it still is. Although Colin used to drop in to the house from time to time, I was not too keen to see him. I was living with my girlfriend,

Veronica, and we had a baby girl. I was all mixed up inside - I didn't know what was happening to me - maybe it was the effect of the drugs. I just didn't know.

It was about six months later that I made a radical decision within my own mind. I wanted to know this God. I invited Jesus into my life. Through him, I am still learning many things about God and the Father's love for me. Veronica soon shared my faith - though we both had to come through quite a lot. Not long afterwards we got married.

But six months before our marriage there was a point where I felt I was at an end regarding my faith. I really felt I had hit a brick wall. When I told Colin he said that, although we had made a Christian commitment, we were still living in a state of sin. It seemed so clear when he explained it, but I could see problems.

'How do I speak to Veronica about this?' I wondered.

That night I told her what I had been thinking. Then she told me she had been to see Frank O'Gara, a Christian friend, that day and they had been discussing the very same thing. Not surprisingly they had reached the same conclusion! So for the next six months we lived as brother and sister - to the amazement of our friends! The more we sought the Lord, the more he drew closer to us. But we had a lot to learn.

On one occasion I read a little book which said: 'Stop denying the fact that you are a son of God, bought and paid for with the blood of Jesus'. That spoke directly to me because I still found it hard to tell people I had made a commitment to Christ, yet I knew I ought to do it.

The following Sunday morning our doorbell went and this guy was standing there asking me if I believed in

God! 'This is a great opportunity,' I thought.

'Yes,' I said. 'I am a son of God through Jesus. Are you?'

'No. I'm a Jehovah's Witness,' he said.

Thinking that here was a possible convert through my witness, I asked him to come in. I admitted I didn't know much about Jehovah's Witnesses and asked him what were the differences between us.

'Do you believe in God the Father?' I asked. He said he did.

'You don't believe in Jesus then?'

'Yes,' he said.

'The Holy Spirit?' I asked.

Again he said, 'Yes.'

'So what's the difference?' I thought.

At that moment the doorbell rang and it was Colin. I quietly told him that I had a Jehovah's Witness in.

'Don't ever let them over your door,' he ordered. 'They bring a spirit of confusion in with them.'

Thinking that 'big Colin' was into all his 'airy fairy' stuff, I showed him into the room.

As soon as he entered Colin said he would pray in Jesus' name. That was it! The Jehovah's Witness said that they were taught that the Father, Son and Holy Ghost were separate.

The truth never really hit me until later that night, but when it did, it bowled me over. And then fear came upon me. I had given my life to Jesus in a Trinity with his Father and his Spirit. I was in tears.

'How could this be?' I wondered. I had never really understood that teaching from the Bible before. From that day on I started at Matthew's Gospel to John's and read it over and over, and still do.

That night I told Veronica what I was feeling and thinking. I cannot remember such dread in all my life. I picked up the Bible and opened it where I had finished reading the night before.

It was in John's Gospel and Philip was asking Jesus to let him see the Father to satisfy his belief. Jesus replied: 'To have seen me is to have seen the Father. Do you not believe that I am in the Father and the Father is in me?'

I felt as if God had opened the doors of heaven and given me a vision beyond all imagination. There were many such blessings at that time - too many to write about.

I became more active with Prison Fellowship. I used to spend Mondays and Thursdays up at their office, meeting different people and helping Colin. Then I would go along to the Saturday night ex-offenders' meeting. At that time no one was really leading the group, although one of the Trustees would come along.

I learnt a lot at those meetings. Sometimes there would only be four or five of us, but it really moved me that men could share with one another in such depth. Then I was asked if I would lead the group, and I did. For the next three years I was blessed at those meetings but in the summer of '91 I had to give it up when our third child arrived.

When I asked Christ into my heart, he showed me that the Christian journey through life is very much an internal journey. In the west of Scotland one of the biggest problems is bigotry within religion. If I bring my children up to think that 'we' are right and 'they' are wrong, then I bring them up with a very narrow vision.

But Jesus comes into our lives to set us free, not to further bind us up by prejudice.

Another area I am beginning to see that men get wrong is in their attitude towards women. Women are seen first and foremost as partners. In marriage it is even more so because we become 'one flesh'. We would all like the idea of love being something that constantly makes us 'feel good', but that is a far-fetched ideal. The reality of love is that it is sometimes a pain in the whatever! Yet in marriage we can get in touch with who we really are, through our partner. At times they can seem a real nag, but if we can get through these times, we can learn a lot about love. When we look at God's love for us in Christ, we see it is completely opposite to our selfish kind of love.

During this period of leading the Saturday night meetings, the Lord showed me that there is something really special in men meeting together in his name. I realised that we all play roles and men come across as being tough and unmovable, especially when women are present. Yet I have been with some of the toughest at their weakest moments and through them I have learnt that the Lord wants us to be true to ourselves and to him.

In prison you don't need anyone to tell you that you are not free. You are one of the first to know! But people who don't get into prison may think they are free when really they are prisoners - emotionally, spiritually or psychologically. I was more of a prisoner outside prison than when I was inside.

I know that, over the past five years, I have been given a vision from the Lord - but I never forget the beginning. I am a sinner, but Jesus saves. He saves us to serve, and the two main areas where he has directed me to serve are offenders and youth. Today I work with young homeless people. You can really feel their thirst for truth. They have given me more than I could ever give them, but they really need men and women who will stand with them in truth.

I look at today's youth and I can see so much abuse - physical, sexual, and from drugs, alcohol, solvents and much more. I believe God is doing something about this. Youngsters today act so much older than when I was their age. Working with them shows me so much. In their sexuality they are experimenting in many ways - yet unless we educate them, this will only continue. We need the Lord's wisdom to speak to the youth of today in words they can relate to and understand.

I hope my story will help you look for the peace that all men and women seek. You need not look further than the cross of Jesus. While I was 'still a long way off', God my Father welcomed me home, just as he did the prodigal son. I transferred my allegiance from the false god, money, to the one true God, and he welcomed me with open arms.

* * * * *

You've read how the key man in Joe's life was Colin Cuthbert. Now read how God apprehended this one-time island farmer and revolutionised his life too ....

> 'I will give you every place where you set your foot,
> as I promised Moses ...' (Joshua 1:3).

17

WALKING THE JOB
by Colin Cuthbert
Director of Prison Fellowship Scotland,
(1987-)

I was a dairy farmer in the parish of St. Ola in Orkney when, in the summer of 1979, Bruce and Sheila Lenman and their family came there on holiday. In our church in Kirkwall, they fell into conversation with my wife, May, and she invited them to visit our farm. From this small start grew a friendship which was to have a tremendous impact on my life - and, without anyone realising it, the seeds of my involvement with Prison Fellowship were sown.

The following summer, the Lenmans invited us to spend a holiday at their home in St. Andrews and to attend a Christian Conference with them. On the third evening of the Conference the speaker, having preached the gospel, asked any who wished, to respond and 'invite Christ into their lives'. That evening I experienced what the Bible calls being 'born again'.

From then on the Holy Spirit made the Bible come alive in a way I had never known before. I felt as if my eyes and ears had been opened! As soon as I got back to Orkney I went to tell my minister what had happened, and

169

along with a few others, we started a small fellowship group which met at the farm on Monday evenings. Then I found that another farmer from the west mainland of Orkney had had a similar experience to my own, and he and his wife also joined our small interdenominational fellowship meeting.

During the following year I began to wonder if God wanted me to stay on as a dairy farmer, or whether he might have other plans for me. I had begun to feel that he might want me to move to Glasgow and study theology at Bible College, but I wasn't sure. The only way to find out was to pray - so I did.

If God wanted us to move, he would need to find a buyer for the farm and all the milking cows, as well as employment for the three men who worked for me. In the summer of 1980, God did just that. A Shetland farmer bought everything, and our family set out for a new life in the city of Glasgow where I was to study theology for the next three years.

One day the College Notice board advertised a Lunchtime Service to be held in St. George's Tron Parish Church in Glasgow, at which Chuck Colson was to be the speaker. I had a strong feeling that I should attend the meeting - though I was the only one from College who did so. Again, in his unique way, God was continuing to prepare me for his future plans.

During my three years at College I attended an independent evangelical church, and I emerged with a conviction that God wanted me to work in some form of interdenominational service. But exactly what I was to do remained a mystery to me! Again I prayed: 'Lord, where do you want me to go now? What do you want me to do?'

As far as I could tell, God remained silent. So for several months I signed on 'the broo' at Springburn and occupied my time helping with the young people in the church.

The following year I got the opportunity to work with children in care in a children's home on the north side of Glasgow. I enjoyed the job very much, but there was one major drawback - the shift system meant that I had to work nights. The dairy farmer who rose at 5.30 a.m. was now being asked to sleep during the day and stay awake at night! I enjoyed working with the children, but I was quite relieved when a new opportunity came along.

I next went to work with mentally handicapped people in the Maryhill district of Glasgow - and it proved to be quite a challenge. The highlight of my time with them was when I went back to Orkney, taking a group of ten adults for a holiday.

For the next year I worked in a drug project which aimed at helping people with drug problems. Part of my job involved visiting 'the clients' who had found their way into prison. Unexpectedly, I found that I felt strangely at home in the prisons - again, no doubt it was God's way of taking me a stage nearer to the goal he had for me.

While visiting Barlinnie in the autumn of 1987, I met Social Worker Angus Creighton. As we were chatting about various things, he mentioned that he was involved in the Prison Fellowship ministry and that they were looking for a full-time worker. I couldn't see that it would affect me, as I was quite happy working in the drugs project. But then, a few days later, Sheila Lenman came to tea. She also mentioned that Prison Fellowship was looking for a full-time worker! Could the Lord be trying to say something to me, I wondered?

The next day was Sunday, and during a time of open worship at church, Linda, a policeman's wife, read from Isaiah 42:3, 'A bruised reed he will not break, and a smouldering wick he shall not snuff out'. On Tuesday a Prison Fellowship application form arrived from Sheila, and when I looked at the stationery, I saw their logo - the 'bruised reed' of Isaiah 42:3! Just to be sure I got the message, one of the elders read Isaiah 42:3 the following Sunday in church!

I needed no more urging - I completed the forms and sent them away.

I felt very nervous when I attended the interview in Edinburgh before a panel of Trustees from Prison Fellowship, who were total strangers to me. But they sensed God's call on my life and appointed me Director. Both my wife and I had peace that this was where God wanted us to be. My involvement with Prison Fellowship had begun!

My commissioning service was held in Perth, led by the Chairman of Prison Fellowship Scotland, and attended by volunteers from all over Scotland. A week later I had to speak about Prison Fellowship to a staff training meeting in Greenock prison, and even though a Christian Governor was directing it, I was all too aware of my lack of experience.

I spent the next few weeks visiting as many Prayer Support Groups and 'in prison' Fellowship teams as possible, as well as volunteers who hadn't been able to attend the service in Perth.

Soon after starting the job I travelled to Ayr to meet Bishop Maurice Taylor. He had been Vice-Chairman of Prison Fellowship in the early days. I had never prayed with a Catholic Bishop before, but I found myself at ease and 'at one' in Christ. Bishop Taylor encouraged me in the task of relating to all branches of the Christian community. He also gave me an opportunity to meet the Principal of Gillies College in Edinburgh.

This pattern of personal contact with brothers and sisters in Christ throughout the country continues to this day. It is God's way of guiding me to friends of all denominations who have a concern for prisons, prisoners and their families. It is an important part of my new 'travelling' lifestyle.

I sometimes cover over 30,000 miles a year - from Orkney in the north to Lewis, Tiree, and Arran in the west; to Newton Stewart, Dumfries and Berwick in the south, and Aberdeen and Peterhead in the north east. The Prison Fellowship cars have all been red ones, with a sticker on the back which reads: 'There is Hope'. When I meet young men who are in prison for car theft, I often ask them if they'd be kind enough to leave that car alone!

Each year I meet with the Director of the Scottish Prison Service, the heads of the Chaplaincy Board and the Governors and Chaplains of every prison where Prison Fellowship is actively supporting the Chaplains. The main ways of assisting the Chaplains are through the weekly Fellowship Groups, Gospel concerts and Fellowship weekends, and follow-up of ex-prisoners upon release.

We have also developed links with other Christian ministries such as the Telephone Prayer Chain, the Lawyers' Christian Fellowship, the Christian Police Association, the Christian Social Workers' Fellowship, the Gideons and the Lydia Intercessors in Glasgow. All

173

these groups maintain close contact with Prison Fellowship in prayer, and support us in many other ways.

On one occasion I invited two members of the Gideons and some members of the Christian Police Association to make a presentation of Gideon New Testaments at Longriggend Remand Institution. There were twenty-four boys in the Bible Class that day and, before making the presentation, Inspector Roy spoke about the origin and work of the Gideons.

As we were leaving the prison, Roy made a confession. 'I didn't like to tell the boys that I was a policeman, as I wasn't sure what would happen!'

Many policemen and ex-policemen have taken part quite openly in our Fellowship groups since then.

Prayer is vital in our ministry and we have continued to set up prayer groups throughout Scotland. A growing number of churches are associated with Prison Fellowship, where Christians from a particular church feel a desire to pray for those in prison. They meet locally and use the National Prayer Card, a local prayer letter, or establish contact with a prison or prisoner.

In the spring of 1987, I was invited by David Connelly, a member of the Prison Social Work team, to attend a Christian Men's Breakfast in Glasgow. The speaker was a Prison Chaplain.

What happened that morning was to prove a pattern for the years to come. I found myself drawn to the man sitting opposite me - David Connelly's brother, Joe. After the Breakfast we chatted and I invited him to come to the Prison Fellowship office the following week for a bite to eat and a chat.

What I didn't realise was that Joe's brother, David,

had been fasting and praying for him for some time. Our meeting was, in fact, to be God's way of touching Joe, as you will have read in the previous chapter. David Connelly has since started a group similar to Prison Fellowship, called simply: 'Hope'.

The countries chartered to Prison Fellowship International meet for a weekend each year in different regions of the world to pray and discuss issues affecting their own particular area.

In the early summer of 1987 we received a call from Northern Ireland from the father of a patient in the State Hospital at Carstairs. He asked if it would be possible for us to visit his son, as they could only travel over infrequently. We agreed to do this, though it was a new experience for those involved in Prison Fellowship. When we arrived we found there were three more patients in Carstairs, who had attended Prison Fellowship in the prisons - and so began what were to become regular visits to Carstairs.

We formed a group of twelve volunteers and visited each patient individually once a month. By November 1989 we had contact with sixteen patients, and, with the Chaplain's help, we started a Fellowship meeting. The number of patients has continued to grow and at present the Hospital Fellowship meeting is held twice a month.

We also arrange one-to-one visits to those patients who don't have regular visitors. As the patients improve and the men and women are transferred back to local psychiatric hospitals or to prison to complete their sentences, we try to link them with volunteers who will keep in touch with them.

Prison Fellowship also tries to help the families of

prisoners in practical ways. Sometimes our volunteers offer accommodation to them when they come from a distance to visit their inmate relatives. Sometimes we are able to provide furniture and clothing to inmates on their release. We also arrange to meet prisoners at the prison gate on their release, often at 6 or 7 a.m. We take them for breakfast and see them off on a train, or perhaps take them to Christian rehabilitation or discipleship Houses or to Volunteers' homes to stay.

Every autumn we hold Volunteer Training Days when we try to teach Volunteers about the various problems and issues which might arise in prison. We invite a variety of professionals to share their expertise with us. After ten years, many of our Volunteers have had first-rate training for their work.

Since May 1987 we have held an Annual Fellowship Day at Bishopbriggs. This day is focused on fellowship and includes speakers from many backgrounds - Prison Governors, Chaplains, ex-offenders, friends from other ministries, Prayer Group leaders and Prison Officers. We also welcome guests from Britain and abroad, ex-offenders, and men presently serving in 'open' or 'semi-open' conditions. In 1987 we had a grandfather from Uganda who had served five prison sentences for preaching the gospel under the reign of Idi Amin!

A Fellowship Weekend is also held every year in Cornton Vale Women's Prison, where Chaplain Sheila organises a Friday evening concert, a Saturday seminar, and a Sunday morning service to which Volunteers are invited. Their speakers have included ex-missionaries, ex-prisoners, ex-drug addicts, ex-alcoholics, ex-spiritualists, Prison Officers, people involved in after-care and other Prison Fellowship Volunteers. The number of girls attending these seminars has varied from eleven to thirty-three, and it has been exciting to see God touch the lives of girls who had never before been to a church service or Bible class.

One prisoner, who was a Christian, felt unable to forgive a close relative. Then, just two days before her release, she finally forgave him. Another girl, who had been a heroin addict for eight years, left prison two days after attending the Fellowship Weekend and committed her life to Christ two weeks later. She went on to a Christian Discipleship House and joined a church in Glasgow.

As God has changed the lives of prisoners and ex-prisoners, some of them have felt that God wanted them to become Prison Fellowship Volunteers, though not all choose to maintain contact. For those who want to be active Volunteers in Prison Fellowship there is a rule that they must first have been out of the prison system for at least two years. They must also have established themselves in a local church, to mature as Christians and to demonstrate that the change in them is permanent. More and more ex-offenders are now part of the teams going into prison on a regular basis. Many more are guests in our fellowship teams. The list is growing and it is a joy to see that now, over ten per cent of our Volunteers are ex-inmates.

Representatives of Prison Fellowship are often invited to speak in churches, and they are usually accompanied by an ex-offender who also takes part in the programme. On one occasion we were invited to speak at an evening service of a Free Church of Scotland and a group of us took part. One preached, another explained about the local Prayer Support group, another spoke about the meeting in prison, and an ex-offender told his story. The ex-offender had served a five year sentence for police assault. After the service was over we were amazed to find that five of the congregation were ex-policemen! God surely has a sense of humour.

For two weeks in 1991 we spent time in fasting and prayer during the Billy Graham Mission to Scotland. All the prisons and the State Hospital were supplied with videos of the event so that they could be shown to interested inmates. Two prisons allowed men to travel to the 'live events' and one prison took the satellite link directly to the Institution to be shown either during the day or in the evening.

In Longriggend Remand Institution, a team of Volunteers from the Chaplain's Department and Prison Fellowship showed the videos both afternoons and evenings. Over 170 boys attended and thirty-three made further enquiries either about committing their lives to Christ or wanting to hear more about the gospel. Some of these boys have become Christians.

At the State Hospital in Carstairs the videos were shown the week after the live event, and posters were displayed in all the wards. Then the chief Security Officer 'phoned to say that he had problems. At first I thought he was going to cancel the event but instead he said that there were so many patients wishing to attend that it was impossible for them all to be together. So we arranged to hold the viewing in two locations for two evenings each. On the first evening, twenty-eight patients attended and when an altar call was made, twenty-four of them came forward to make enquiry about the Christian life. At the end of the week, forty patients had expressed their interest.

Prayer has been and remains the main focus of Prison Fellowship and its Volunteers. The number of groups meeting to pray continues to rise steadily as more and more Christians in Scotland indicate their wish to pray for prisons.

Their prayers are for Governors and Staff, as well as inmates and their families. They also pray for victims of crime and their families. We send individual prayer cards to over three thousand friends throughout Scotland, encouraging them to pray at 12 noon, when the hands of the clock come together, and to fast on Tuesdays. This pattern has been adopted by Prison Fellowship International, and today continuous prayer is reaching heaven on behalf of those in prison and those involved in prison ministry.

At one point we were burdened to pray three mornings in a row for those who were suicidal in prison. Later in the week we heard that there had been three attempted suicides that week - but that all three prisoners were alive and well!

One evening the Edinburgh prayer group were meeting when a Prison Works Officer was taken hostage and threatened by inmates. They spent the whole evening interceding for this situation. It was a joy to see the Officer appear on television the following evening to say that he was prepared to go back to work within the next few days. God does hear and answer prayers.

Today, more and more people are meeting with Christ both in prison and after their release. The change in their lives is remarked upon by relatives and friends so that they, in turn, are challenged by the claims of Christ. I feel blessed 'walking the job' and pray that God 'will give us every place we set our feet', as he promised Joshua centuries ago.

* * * * *

A few final thoughts from Louise ...

> 'We constantly pray for you...'
> (2 Thessalonians 1:11)

18

PRAYER IS THE KEY
by Louise Purvis

The prayerful example of Prison Fellowship in England, combined with our own deep fellowship in the core group, showed us that prayer was the key - the key to finding out God's agenda; the key to testing motivation, staying power and Christian maturity; the key to defeating the evil 'principalities and powers' mentioned in the Bible; the key to preparing the hearts of both volunteers and inmates before our in-prison activities; the key to making divine appointments between volunteers and inmates; the key to working in the hearts of inmates where Christian volunteers were not visiting; the key to uniting in Christ the volunteers going into prison.

But we soon discovered that prayer is not a soft option - nor the easiest way to find volunteers! It was quite the opposite. We had access to many prisons from the outset, and many Christians were eager to go into the prisons, so prayer was not a tactic for keeping people busy until the prison gates were opened to us. But the requirement that our volunteers meet regularly for prayer certainly sorted out the sheep from the goats!

This was important, because ours was not a ministry for faint hearts who would not stick the course. We didn't want large numbers of volunteers, but just those whom God had truly called and who were committed to working with us.

We knew that prayer would lead to care, the other most important aspect of our ministry. Prayer and care are partners, opposite sides of the same coin, and mutually interdependent. We knew then, as we know now, that one without the other was incomplete, and that care which stems from prayer is of a different quality altogether.

I confess that, even after all this time, I still don't understand the dynamic of prayer. However, an English Prison Chaplain gave as good an explanation as I've ever heard. He wrote: 'Outside the walls, Christians can pray. If people prayed for prisoners as often as they condemned them, we might have a more just and humane society. Prayer digs tunnels into prisons. It undermines the walls that divide us. It awakens our imagination and concern. It is God's messenger that may speak in the silence of the cell - and prisoners have acute spiritual hearing. It brings to mind the faceless and the forgotten, and the forgotten do not forget those who remember them.'[1]

It is ironic that, while most people think of tunnelling out of prison, our volunteers spend their time tunnelling in through prayer!

It is important to stress here that our volunteers never condone the crimes of the men and women we pray for. Our sympathy is entirely with the victims of crime. In fact in many countries Prison Fellowship runs Victim Support schemes.

---

1. Rev. Harry Potter, Chaplain of Aylesbury Prison. With kind permission.

But while we hate the sin, we must continue to love the sinner, as God continues to love us. By offering offenders an alternative Christian life-style, we hope that they will never again consider rape, robbery or murder. Nobody can be committed to Christ and to crime at the same time. So by helping and praying for offenders, we are also helping to reduce the number of crimes and victims.

In order to do this we try to deal with the root cause of the crime, not just the symptoms. If taking drink and drugs leads to crime, we must obviously try to get people off drink and drugs. But taking these substances is itself only a symptom of deeper problems. The pain which arises from insecurity, lack of love, self-esteem or purpose leads to escapism. Unless the reasons for this pain are dealt with, drinking and drug-taking continue and the cycle is perpetuated.

Therefore, understanding how much one is loved by God is often the cure - the breakthrough - for inmates, as for all our volunteers. Being deeply loved provides security, self-esteem and purpose in living. And the guidelines for 'right living' are all set out in the Bible. There is no issue which is not dealt with in its pages. So when we tell men and women about the gospel, we are offering them something with which to solve life's deepest problems. Their problems won't go away, but their ability to deal with their problems will be greatly strengthened.

Over the years I have seen how the power of prayer has literally changed lives in our prisons. I have witnessed quite inexplicable happenings: one of Scotland's most notorious criminals shaking hands and forgiving his arch-enemy, a man he believed responsible for his nephew's death; another of Scotland's 'tough guys', converted as he listened to a volunteer sing 'One day at a time, sweet Jesus'; a Young Offender also converted because a motherly volunteer touched his arm and told him of the goodness she saw in him.

These things would never have happened without prayer. This prayer, combined with the love God gives our volunteers for the inmates, is the most powerful force in the world - the only power strong enough to break the cycle of hate and evil.

As we pray for people, we begin to love them. And when love comes face to face with the hurt and need in prisoners, backed by prayer, something extraordinary happens. For some inmates, it is their first experience ever of receiving unconditional love. It bowls them over, and it opens up a new life in Christ for many.

So when we ask our volunteers to be involved in prayer, we do it in the belief that there is exactly where the battle will be won or lost.

Some of our prayer support groups have been meeting for ten years and are only now beginning to see big results. Their faithfulness in prayer must have touched God's heart.

The mixture of people in our prayer groups must also make God smile - doctors and ex-drug addicts, judges and ex-prisoners, titled ladies and ex-prostitutes, prisoners and prison officers, children and grandparents, Catholics and Protestants, politicians and policemen. I often think this cross-section of society who meet to pray might be a small foretaste of what heaven will be like.

Will you be there?

* * * * *

Looking back over the first ten years of Prison Fellowship many memories stand out: the early meetings with Prison Governors and church leaders; the tours with Sylvia Mary Alison, Chuck Colson and distinguished ex-prisoners, Fred Lemon, Rita Nightingale, Tony Ralls and ex-terrorist David 'Packy' Hamilton; the Fellowship weekends in prisons; the visits in my home by prisoners, ex-prisoners and their families; the inmates who ministered to us when John was defeated in the 1984 Euro-election.

What has impressed me most, however, is the sacrificial commitment of our volunteers; the prison officers and staff who come back into prison for Fellowship meetings after a double shift; the prison visitors who miss tea and travel for an hour by bus after work to reach the prison; the families who open their homes to homeless ex-prisoners when they have barely enough to eat themselves; the volunteers who wait at the prison gate at 6.00 a.m. to welcome prisoners back into the community; those who provide and move furniture into ex-prisoner's flats in all weathers; who drive ex-prisoners to drug 'rehabs' in London on Christmas Eve; the people who have given up weekends and holidays for training; who have never claimed expenses; who have kept attending 'in-prison' Fellowships when numbers were low; the growing number of ex-prisoner volunteers who are willing to go back into prison; and, of course, our inmate volunteers, whose courage and faithfulness have kept us all going.

Without all these, Prison Fellowship would not exist. But with them, and by God's grace, we look forward to the next ten years.

Epilogue

WE KNEW YOU WOULD COME

by Louise Purvis,
Vice-Chairman of Prison Fellowship

Many of you reading this book may not believe in miracles. But to me, this book is full of miracles - the greatest miracle of all being the change in men's hearts and minds and lives, from 'self-centred' to 'God-centred'. All of us writing in this book have been set free by such a change. Some who are still in prison are the freest men and women I know.

But the vast majority of men and women are still in their various prisons and chains. To you I can only say, 'You know we'll keep coming'.

You know we'll keep coming out of love and gratitude for what God has done in our own lives.

You know we'll keep coming because prisoners are very much on God's heart and God's agenda.

You know we'll keep coming because Jesus' job description for himself and us was 'to preach Good News to the poor and to proclaim freedom for the prisoners'.

You know we'll keep coming because Jesus has invited us into prison.

You know we'll keep coming because we see the potential for Jesus in every human being.

You know we'll keep coming because we have love

and compassion for the victims of crime and want to see fewer of them.

You know we'll keep coming in our visits and groups and letters and books and Bibles and cassettes and videos and, most of all, in our prayers.

And when we come, we will come humbly, knowing that we too might still be in prison but for the love of God.

We come as children of God, brothers and sisters of Jesus, the whole Body of Christ outside prison to the whole Body of Christ inside prison.

We come with the help and guidance and power of the Holy Spirit indwelling us.

We come on the wings of the prayers of thousands of unseen volunteers who are continually 'tunnelling into prison' in prayer.

We come, overflowing with God's love to those we meet inside, and are blessed by the love which flows back to us.

We come as Jesus' hands and feet and voice and heart to 'the least of these his brothers', and as he promised, we find Jesus himself, serving a 'Life Sentence'.

We come with the 'Good News' that has set so many men and women free. The gospel message we bring is personal. It is practical. It is positive. It is psychologically sound. And it works. The stories in this book are living proof of that. All the stories show that God loves us long before we love him. He loves us before we become good. The Bible says: 'While we were still sinners, Christ died for us'. What's more, there is nothing we can do to make God love us more or make him love us less. We can break his heart, of course, like children who break their parents' hearts. But he loves us anyway.

How much did he love us? He sent us his Son, who stretched out his arms on a cross and said 'This much', and died.

But while we can offer the gospel message to men and women in prison, in the end the choice is theirs. Some will choose to accept it - some will choose to reject it. It's always been the same. One thief on the cross next to Jesus rejected his claims. The other accepted them. He is now in paradise with Jesus.

The claims of Christ still demand a choice to accept or reject him. He will never force our choice. But in that choice hangs all the difference between life and death; hope and despair; peace or fear; security or insecurity; belonging or loneliness; purpose or meaninglessness; power or helplessness; love or lack of it.

I wonder if you who read this, have made that choice? It could change your life, as it has changed all of ours. We were all in prisons, with or without bars, but Christ set us free.

* * * * *

Chuck Colson once told us the moving story of paying an unexpected visit to an inmate on Death Row early one Easter morning. When he arrived, Chuck was surprised that the prisoner was up and dressed and waiting. Chuck apologised anyway for not letting the inmate know of his visit in advance, but the inmate only smiled, and said: 'That's alright, Chuck. I knew you would come.'

Since hearing that story, our prayer has been that the inmates of Scotland would say of God's people in Scotland: 'We knew you would come.'

PRISON FELLOWSHIP *SCOTLAND*

If you are an inmate, ex-inmate or relation, or are interested in becoming a Prison Fellowship Volunteer, you can receive further information by writing to or telephoning:

Colin Cuthbert
Director of Prison Fellowship Scotland
P.O. Box 366
Glasgow
G22 5QS
Tel: 041-332-8870

or
Prison Fellowship England and Wales
P.O. Box 945
Chelmsford
Essex CM2 7PX
Tel:0245-490-249

or
Prison Fellowship Northern Ireland
39 University Street,
Belfast BT7 1FY
Northern Ireland
Tel:0232 243691